simply *Cadbury's*
chocolate

simply *Cadbury's* chocolate

Joanna Farrow

hamlyn

Executive Editor: Polly Manguel
Editor: Katey Day
Art Director: Keith Martin
Senior Designer: Leigh Jones
Senior Production Controller: Katherine Hockley

Contributors
Photographer: Ian Wallace
Home Economist: Joanna Farrow
Stylist: Claire Hunt
Picture Researcher: Christine Junemann
Indexer: Hilary Bird

Simply Cadbury's Chocolate by Joanna Farrow

First published in 1999 by Hamlyn
an imprint of Octopus Publishing Group Limited
2–4 Heron Quays, London E14 4JP

British Library Cataloguing-in-Publication Data
A catalogue record for this book is available from the British Library

ISBN 0 600 598276

Printed in China

Notes
Recipes using Cadbury's Flake use the standard size bars, but Cadbury's Flake from a '99' family box may also be used. If using Cadbury's Flake from a '99' family box, use twice the number stated in the recipe to allow for their smaller size.

Standard level spoon measurements are used in all recipes.
1 tablespoon = one 15 ml spoon
1 teaspoon = one 5 ml spoon

Both imperial and metric measurements have been given in all recipes. Use one set of measurements only and not a mixture of both.

Eggs should be medium (size 3) unless otherwise stated.

Ovens should be preheated to the specified temperature – if using a fan assisted oven, follow the manufacturer's instructions for adjusting the time and temperature.

This book includes dishes made with nuts and nut derivatives. It is advisable for customers with known allergic reactions to nuts and nut derivatives and those who may be potentially vulnerable to these allergies, such as pregnant and nursing mothers, invalids, the elderly, babies and children, to avoid dishes made with nuts and nut oils. It is also prudent to check the labels of pre-prepared ingredients for the possible inclusion of nut derivatives.

contents

introduction

Since its introduction to Europe several centuries ago, the rich colour, unique texture, tempting aroma and delicious flavour of chocolate have provided us with one of the most irresistible and ever-popular foods. Whether you are making a few cookies or a large luscious gâteau, chocolate is the one ingredient guaranteed to set your taste buds quivering with anticipation.

The chocolate we enjoy today has been refined and improved out of recognition since it was first discovered by the Maya, an ancient people of Central America, in the rainforests of the Amazon. The Maya used cocoa beans not only to make a drink called *chocolatl,* but also as a form of currency. In this way, the secret of *chocolatl* was passed to the Aztecs of Mexico, who valued it so highly that it is said the conquering Spaniard Don Cortez was served *chocolatl*, then drunk cold, mixed with ground maize and flavoured with vanilla and chillies, in a golden goblet at the court of the Emperor Montezuma.

Chocolate crossed the Atlantic to Europe in the 1520s soon after the Spanish had conquered Mexico. The European version which reached Britain in the 1650s was an expensive luxury, sold (now served hot and without the chillies) at the newly established London chocolate houses. It was not until Victorian times, when processes for making solid blocks of eating chocolate had been perfected, that chocolate was used other than as a drink. Indeed, when John Cadbury first began to sell chocolate in 1824, it was sold as a delicious, nutritious breakfast drink. By 1849 Cadbury had perfected a technique for making bars of chocolate and the chocolate we enjoy today was born.

Cadbury's chocolate Easter eggs first appeared in 1875 and Cadbury's Dairy Milk chocolate, made with fresh milk and superior in taste and texture to the coarse and dry milk chocolate then available, dates from 1905. Cadbury's Bournville, the smooth dark chocolate named after the company's 'factory in a garden' in Birmingham, was launched in 1908.

Above: The cocoa tree, *theobroma cacao,* the source of both cocoa and chocolate. The tree is about the size of an apple tree, while the pods which contain the beans are about 15–20 cm (6–8 inches) long.

The history of Cadbury, however, is more than just a story of industrial and marketing success. The Cadbury family were members of the Society of Friends, the Quakers, a nonconformist religious group whose high moral ideals were put into practice through social reforms. After John Cadbury's sons, Richard and George, took over the business in 1861, it became so successful that they were able to turn their attention to making practical improvements to their workers lives. In 1879, work began on their new factory in the countryside just outside Birmingham. With its adjacent garden village complete with spacious well-designed houses, wide streets, playing fields and libraries for their employees, Bournville was a green and pleasant land in contrast to the slums of Birmingham.

Above and left: Early examples of Cadbury's packaging, including the first Cadbury's Dairy Milk pack from 1905.

Manufacturing Chocolate

The cocoa tree, which flourishes in humid tropical climates with regular rains and a short dry season, is still grown in Central and South America, although today West Africa is the world's major cocoa producer, with Ghana producing high-quality cocoa. A tree produces about 20–30 pods a year, each containing about 30–40 cocoa beans buried amongst its soft pulpy fibres. Surprisingly, the annual crop from one tree is only enough to make 500 g (1 lb) of cocoa. Once harvested, the cocoa beans are fermented then left to dry before being shipped abroad. When they reach the cocoa processing factories the beans are cleaned and roasted to develop chocolate's wonderful aroma and flavour. The beans are then crushed and the centres ground until they become liquid. This liquid, known as mass or cocoa liquor, is the basic ingredient for all chocolate products.

Below: The Village Green at Bournville.

Chocolate Decorations

These decorations can make the perfect finishing touch for your special chocolate desserts and gâteaux. They can be made up to two weeks in advance and stored in an airtight container in a cool place. If the chocolate is brittle and crumbles when you attempt to make chocolate curls or caraque, it may be too cold. If this is so, leave it for a while at room temperature to soften slightly.

Melting Chocolate

Many of the recipes in this book include melted chocolate. This is quite easy, as long as you take time and care. Plain chocolate is usually easier to melt than milk chocolate as it has a lower fat content and will not burn as easily, though the technique used applies to both – gentle heat and minimal stirring.

Bring a saucepan of water to a low simmer. Break the chocolate into squares and put them into a heatproof bowl over the simmering water, taking care not to let the bowl touch the water and ensuring that the steam can not escape between the bowl and the saucepan. Remove the pan from the heat and allow the trapped steam to warm the bowl and gently melt the chocolate. A 200 g bar of Cadbury's Bournville can take as long as 10 minutes to melt, but don't stir it until it has melted all the way through. Take care not to over-stir the chocolate or you may destroy its delicate balance of colour, flavour and texture. Use the melted chocolate immediately. You will find that it remains soft if you keep it in a warm place while you are working with it.

You can also use a microwave to melt chocolate. Simply break the chocolate into squares and place them in a 600 ml/1 pint bowl and microwave for 3–4 minutes on the Defrost setting. The time needed will vary according to the thickness of the chocolate and the power of your microwave, so keep an eye on the chocolate as it melts.

Chocolate Caraque

Melt 150 g/5 oz plain, milk or white chocolate with 25 g/1 oz plain, milk or

Above: Chocolate caraque.
Left: Making white chocolate shavings.
Above right: Making a grease-proof paper piping bag.
Far right above: Piping chocolate shapes.
Far right: The finished shapes

white chocolate-flavoured cake covering, and spread on to a clean, smooth surface. When just set, draw a fine-bladed knife across the chocolate at an angle of 45°.

Chocolate Curls

Spread the chocolate on to a clean, smooth surface. When just set, push a clean wallpaper scraper across the surface to make the curls. Mini-curls can be made by using a narrower scraper.

Quick Chocolate Curls

Allow a large bar of plain, milk or white chocolate to soften in a warm room. Using a vegetable peeler, shave off curls.

Chocolate Shavings

Thoroughly wash and dry a 250 g/8 oz margarine tub or similar-sized container. Melt 300 g/10 oz plain or white chocolate with 50 g/2 oz plain or white chocolate-flavoured cake covering. Turn into the tub and leave until set but not hard. Press the chocolate out of the tub. Holding the slab of chocolate in one hand with kitchen paper (to prevent the heat of your hands melting the chocolate), pare off thin shavings with a knife.

Double Chocolate Shavings

Melt 150 g/5 oz white chocolate with 25 g/1 oz white chocolate-flavoured cake covering and turn into the tub as above. Melt 150 g/5 oz plain or milk chocolate with 25 g/1 oz plain or milk chocolate-

flavoured cake covering and spoon over the white chocolate. Set and shape the chocolate as above.

Piping Bags and Nozzles

Greaseproof paper piping bags are much cleaner and easier to use for chocolate work than nylon ones and are frequently used for chocolate decorations. You can either cut off 1 cm/½ inch from the tip of the piping bag and fit a metal piping nozzle, or snip off the merest tip for line piping. For convenience, make up several bags at a time (see below).

To Make a Greaseproof Paper Piping Bag

Halve a 20 cm/8 inch square of grease-proof paper diagonally. With the longest side away from you, fold the right-hand point over to the point nearest you, to make a cone. Fold the left-hand point over the cone so that all four points meet. Fold the points over several times to secure.

Piped Chocolate Shapes

Line a tray with nonstick greaseproof paper. Melt a little plain or white chocolate and place in a paper piping bag. Snip off the merest tip. Pipe simple decorative motifs on to the paper. Leave to set, then peel the paper away from the chocolate.

quick and easy desserts

Just what every busy cook needs, this chapter contains a selection of simple but impressive desserts that really are quick and easy. Most of them can be put together in 20 minutes or even less time, and chilled in the refrigerator until you want them, or baked in the oven while you enjoy your main course.

Little Chocolate Pots

These velvet-smooth chocolate creams make a perfect, make-ahead treat to round off a special supper or lunch. You can serve them alone, or with little dessert biscuits. Keep the leftover egg whites for making meringues.

Serves: **6–8**

Preparation time: 15 minutes, plus cooling and chilling

Cooking time: about 1 hour

600 ml/1 pint single cream
250 g/8 oz Cadbury's Bournville chocolate, broken into pieces
1 egg
4 egg yolks
25 g/1 oz caster sugar
lightly whipped cream or crème fraîche
cocoa powder, for dusting

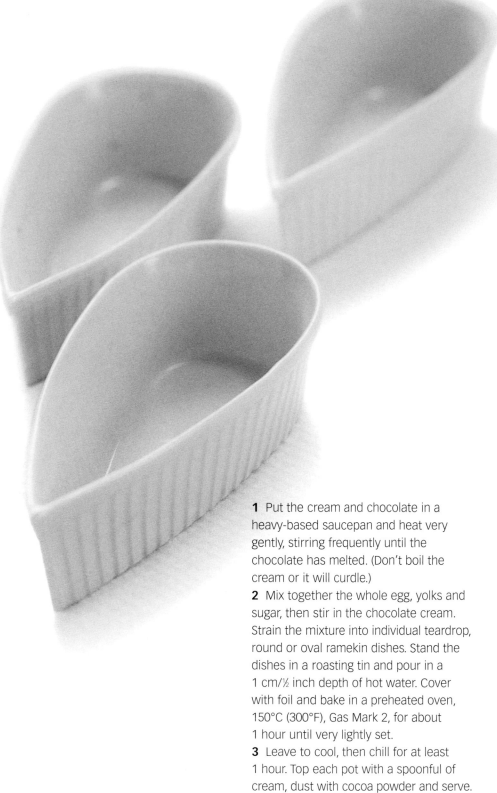

1 Put the cream and chocolate in a heavy-based saucepan and heat very gently, stirring frequently until the chocolate has melted. (Don't boil the cream or it will curdle.)

2 Mix together the whole egg, yolks and sugar, then stir in the chocolate cream. Strain the mixture into individual teardrop, round or oval ramekin dishes. Stand the dishes in a roasting tin and pour in a 1 cm/½ inch depth of hot water. Cover with foil and bake in a preheated oven, 150°C (300°F), Gas Mark 2, for about 1 hour until very lightly set.

3 Leave to cool, then chill for at least 1 hour. Top each pot with a spoonful of cream, dust with cocoa powder and serve.

Zucotto

This is a quick and easy version of an Italian trifle-like dessert, using sherry-steeped chocolate sponge, cream, nuts and of course, plenty of chopped chocolate. Use homemade chocolate sponge or, to speed things up, bought chocolate-chip muffins.

Serves: **6**

Preparation time: 10 minutes

175 g/6 oz chocolate chip muffins
75 ml/3 fl oz orange juice
6 tablespoons medium sherry
25 g/1 oz chopped mixed nuts, toasted
100 g/3½ oz Cadbury's Bournville chocolate, finely chopped
100 g/3½ oz Cadbury's Dairy Milk chocolate, finely chopped
300 ml/½ pint double cream
2 tablespoons caster sugar
½ teaspoon vanilla essence

1 Break up the muffins and divide the pieces among 6 individual serving glasses or put them into 1 large bowl. Drizzle with the orange juice and 4 tablespoons of the sherry.
2 Reserve 2 tablespoons each of the nuts and plain and milk chocolate, then scatter the remainder over the muffins. Lightly whip the cream with the sugar, vanilla and remaining sherry and spoon the mixture over the chocolate. Last, scatter the reserved nuts and chocolate over the top and chill until ready to serve.

Fudge Cheesecake

Most unbaked cheesecakes are set with gelatine, but because this one's so chocolatey, it sets naturally to a lovely thick, fudge-like texture.

Serves: **10**

Preparation time: 15 minutes, plus chilling

Cooking time: 5 minutes

175 g/6 oz chocolate digestive biscuits
40 g/1½ oz unsalted butter
300 g/10 oz Cadbury's Bournville chocolate, broken into pieces
200 g/7 oz cream cheese
250 g/8 oz quark
150 ml/¼ pint double cream
75 g/3 oz icing sugar

1 Line the side of a greased 20 cm/8 inch springform cake tin with greaseproof paper. Put the biscuits in a polythene bag and crush them using a rolling pin. Melt the butter in a saucepan and stir in the crushed biscuits until they are combined. Press the mixture into the base of the prepared tin.
2 Melt 275 g/9 oz of the chocolate. Beat the cream cheese with the quark to soften. Beat in the chocolate, cream and icing sugar until evenly combined. Turn the mixture into the tin and smooth the surface. Chill for at least 3 hours until set.
3 To decorate, melt the remaining chocolate and put it in a piping bag fitted with a fine nozzle. Remove the cheese-cake from the tin and transfer lo a plate. Scribble lines of chocolate over the top.

Banoffi Creams

Flavoured with a whipped blend of toffee yogurt, chocolate Cadbury's Flake and cream, this 5 minute pudding has great kids' appeal.

Serves: **4**

Preparation time: 10 minutes

Cooking time: 5 minutes

75 g/3 oz Cadbury's Dairy Milk chocolate
4 tablespoons milk
2 x 150 ml/¼ pint pots low-fat toffee yogurt
150 ml/¼ pint double cream
2 small ripe bananas
1 Cadbury's Flake

1 Chop the milk chocolate and melt it with the milk in a bowl over a pan of simmering water. Stir gently, then remove from the heat and stir in the yogurt.
2 Lightly whip the cream. Slice the bananas. Cut the Flake lengthways into thick shards. Set aside about one-quarter of the pieces. Layer the chocolate and yogurt mixture, bananas, Flake and cream in serving glasses, finishing with a layer of cream. Scatter with the reserved pieces of Flake.

Chocolate Caramel Custard

Once you've made the caramel, this dessert can be assembled in minutes. It tastes best chilled for several hours before serving.

Serves: **6**

Preparation time: 20 minutes, plus chilling

Cooking time: 5 minutes

100 g/3½ oz caster sugar
250 g/8 oz mascarpone cheese
200 ml/7 fl oz ready-made custard
150 g/5 oz Cadbury's Bournville chocolate
20 sponge fingers
150 ml/¼ pint strong black coffee
cocoa powder, for dusting

1 Lightly oil a baking sheet. Put half the sugar in a small, heavy-based saucepan with 4 tablespoons water. Heat gently until the sugar dissolves. Bring to the boil and boil rapidly until the syrup has turned to a caramel colour. Immediately pour the caramel on to the oiled baking sheet and leave until brittle, about 20 minutes.
2 Using the end of a rolling pin, break the caramel into small pieces. Beat the mascarpone in a bowl with the custard and remaining sugar until smooth. Stir in the caramel. Chop the chocolate into small pieces and add to the bowl.

3 Dip 10 of the sponge fingers into the coffee, then lay them in a shallow serving dish. Spread half the custard mixture over the top. Dip the rest of the sponge fingers in the remaining coffee and arrange them over the custard. Cover with the remaining custard.
4 Level the surface and dust generously with cocoa powder. Chill for several hours until ready to serve.

Chocolate Marble Cheesecake

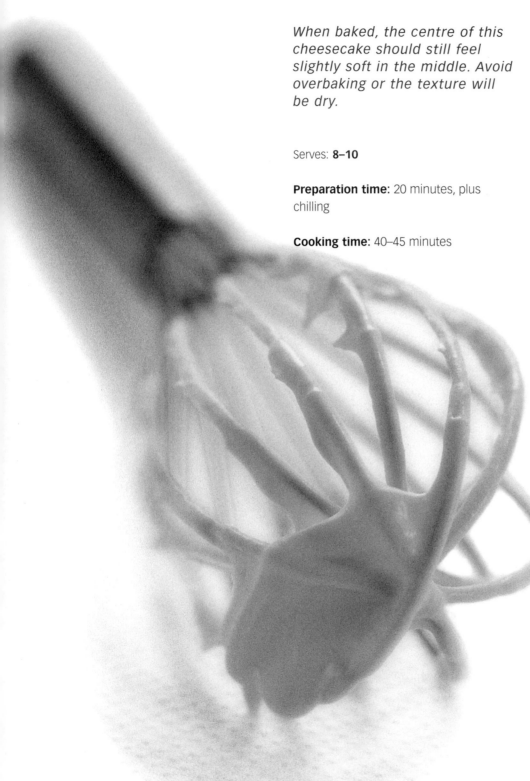

When baked, the centre of this cheesecake should still feel slightly soft in the middle. Avoid overbaking or the texture will be dry.

Serves: **8–10**

Preparation time: 20 minutes, plus chilling

Cooking time: 40–45 minutes

125 g/4 oz gingersnap biscuits
2 tablespoons cocoa powder
40 g/1½ oz unsalted butter
FILLING
400 g/13 oz cream cheese
150 g/5 oz caster sugar
3 eggs
2 teaspoons vanilla essence
150 ml/¼ pint double cream
200 g/7 oz Cadbury's Bournville chocolate,
  broken into pieces
pouring cream, to serve

1 Put the biscuits in a polythene bag and crush them with a rolling pin. Mix the crushed biscuits with the cocoa powder. Melt the butter in a small saucepan and stir in the biscuit mixture until combined. Press the mixture into the base of a 20 cm/8 inch springform cake tin.

2 Beat the cream cheese to soften, then beat in the sugar, eggs, vanilla essence and cream. Melt the chocolate. Spoon about one-third of the cream cheese mixture into a separate bowl and beat in the chocolate.

3 Pour the cream cheese mixture into the tin, then place spoonfuls of the cream cheese and chocolate mixture over it. Using a knife, swirl the mixtures together lightly to create a marbled effect.

4 Bake in a preheated oven, 160°C (325°F), Gas Mark 3, for 35–40 minutes or until the centre of the cheesecake feels only just set. Turn off the oven and leave the cheesecake to cool in it, then transfer to the refrigerator. Serve chilled with pouring cream.

The Best Chocolate Mousse

There are countless recipes for chocolate mousse, some very rich, some bitter, others too sweet and sickly. This one strikes the perfect balance.

Serves: **6**

Preparation time: 15 minutes, plus chilling

Cooking time: 5 minutes

200 g/7 oz Cadbury's Bournville chocolate, broken into pieces
25 g/1 oz unsalted butter, melted
3 tablespoons orange-flavoured liqueur, brandy or rum
150 ml/¼ pint double cream
3 egg whites
2 tablespoons caster sugar
cocoa powder, for dusting

1 Melt the chocolate, then stir in the butter until melted and the liqueur, brandy or rum. Stir gently until smooth. Lightly whip the cream.
2 Whisk the egg whites in a separate bowl until peaking. Whisk in the sugar.
3 Fold the cream, then the egg whites into the melted chocolate mixture, using a large metal spoon, until evenly combined. Turn the mousse into small ramekin dishes or glasses and chill for at least 2 hours until set. Serve dusted with cocoa powder.

Coconut Velvet Tart

This absolutely delicious dessert has a velvety smooth texture because it is made with coconut milk rather than desiccated or grated coconut. For a shortcut version, you can use bought dessert pastry instead of the homemade chocolate one.

Serves: **10–12**

Preparation time: 20 minutes, plus chilling

Cooking time: 45 minutes

150 g/5 oz plain flour
25 g/1 oz cocoa powder
75 g/3 oz unsalted butter
15 g/½ oz caster sugar
1 egg yolk
about 5 teaspoons cold water

FILLING
3 eggs
50 g/2 oz caster sugar
25 g /1 oz cocoa powder
15 g/½ oz cornflour
400 ml/14 fl oz coconut milk
200 g/7 oz Cadbury's Bournville chocolate, broken into pieces
300 ml/½ pint double cream
TO DECORATE
300 ml/½ pint double cream
cocoa powder, for dusting

1 For the pastry, put the flour and cocoa powder in a food processor with the butter and blend until the mixture resembles fine breadcrumbs. Add the sugar, egg yolk and enough water to mix to a firm dough. Chill for 30 minutes.
2 Roll out the pastry and use it to line a 20 cm/8 inch round loose-based flan tin. Line the pastry with greaseproof paper and baking beans and bake in a pre-heated oven, 180°C (350°F), Gas Mark 4, for 15 minutes. Remove the paper and beans and bake the pastry case for a further 5 minutes. Reduce the oven temperature to 150°C (300°F), Gas Mark 2.
3 For the filling, beat together the eggs, sugar and cocoa powder. Put the cornflour in a pan with a little of the coconut milk and stir until smooth. Add the remaining coconut milk and the chocolate. Heat until the chocolate has melted. Bring to the boil, stirring, then pour into the egg mixture, whisking well. Stir in the cream.
4 Turn the mixture into the pastry case and bake for about 25 minutes until the centre feels very softly set. Leave to cool.
5 To decorate, whip the cream until softly peaking and spoon over the tart. Dust lightly with cocoa powder.

Chocolate Cream Dip

This is the nearest you can get to serving neat chocolate for dessert. Melted chocolate, cream and a dash of liqueur, are combined and served in little dishes with biscuits, nuts and fruit for dipping.

Serves: **4**

Preparation time: 5 minutes

Cooking time: 5 minutes

200 g/7 oz Cadbury's Bournville chocolate, broken into pieces
4 tablespoons double cream
4 tablespoons orange-flavoured liqueur
FOR DIPPING
selection of dippers, for example, dessert biscuits, amaretti or cigarette wafer biscuits, biscotti, Brazil nuts, cherries or strawberries, banana slices, dried apricots or mangoes

1 Melt the chocolate with the cream and liqueur, then stir until smooth. Pour into ramekin dishes or other small dishes.
2 Surround with a selection of biscuits, nuts and fruit, plus wooden cocktail sticks for securing the fruit. Serve warm.

Chocolate and Oatmeal Flummery

Toasted oatmeal has a delicious nutty flavour that works really well in creamy desserts. With the addition of apricots, whisky, yogurt and plenty of grated Cadbury's Bournville chocolate, it makes a quick and easy pud.

Serves: **4**

Preparation time: 5 minutes, plus chilling

Cooking time: 2 minutes

25 g/1 oz medium oatmeal
75 g/3 oz ready-to-eat dried apricots
100 g/3½ oz Cadbury's Bournville chocolate
150 ml/¼ pint double cream
25 g/1 oz icing sugar
3 tablespoons whisky
200 g/7 oz Greek yogurt
chocolate curls, to decorate (see page 8)

1 Lightly toast the oatmeal under a warm grill and leave to cool. Finely slice the apricots, then grate the chocolate.
2 Whip the cream in a bowl with the icing sugar and whisky until just beginning to hold its shape. Stir in the yogurt, oatmeal, apricots and chocolate. Turn the mixture into serving glasses. Serve chilled, decorated with chocolate curls.

Caramel Chocolate Rice Castles

aA clever creation, combining creamy rice pudding with chocolate and caramel. Use dariole moulds or individual metal pudding moulds to shape the castles, or small ramekin dishes.

Serves: **6**

Preparation time: 20 minutes, plus cooling

Cooking time: about 1 hour

150 g/5 oz pudding rice
450 ml/¾ pint milk
1 teaspoon vanilla essence
50 g/2 oz caster sugar
125 g/4 oz Cadbury's Bournville chocolate, chopped
3 egg yolks
150 ml/¼ pint double cream
pouring cream or vanilla custard, to serve (optional)
CARAMEL
175 g/6 oz granulated sugar
2 tablespoons water

1 Put the rice, milk, vanilla and sugar in a heavy-based saucepan and bring to the boil. Reduce the heat, cover and simmer gently for about 20 minutes, stirring occasionally until the rice is just tender and most of the liquid is absorbed.
2 Stir in 100 g/3½ oz of the chocolate until melted. Whisk the egg yolks with the cream and stir into the rice.
3 Preheat the oven to 180°C (350°F), Gas Mark 4. For the caramel, put the granulated sugar in a small heavy-based saucepan with the water. Heat very gently until the sugar dissolves. Bring to the boil and boil rapidly until the syrup has turned to a pale caramel colour. Stir in 2 tablespoons water (standing back as the caramel will splutter slightly) and cook until the caramel has softened again.
4 Pour the caramel into 6 small moulds, tilting them so it coats the sides. Spoon in the rice mixture. Place the moulds in a roasting tin and pour in sufficient hot water to come halfway up the sides of the moulds. Bake for 20 minutes until the rice feels only just set. Leave to cool.
5 Melt the remaining chocolate and, using a fine nozzle, scribble lines over 6 serving plates. Loosen the edges of the puddings with a knife, then invert the castles on to serving plates. Serve with pouring cream or custard, if liked.

Chocolate and Raspberry Brulée

Mascarpone cheese has a smooth and creamy texture that goes so well with chocolate. Use Cadbury's Bournville or Cadbury's Dairy Milk chocolate and fresh or frozen raspberries.

Serves: **4**

Preparation time: 2 minutes, plus chilling

Cooking time: 8–10 minutes

250 g/8 oz mascarpone cheese
1 teaspoon vanilla essence
100 g/3½ oz Cadbury's Bournville or Cadbury's Dairy Milk chocolate
4 tablespoons single cream
200 g/7 oz raspberries, thawed if frozen
75 g/3 oz caster sugar

1 Beat the mascarpone cheese with the vanilla essence until smooth. Grate half the chocolate and add to the mixture.

2 Melt the remaining chocolate with the cream. Spoon half the mascarpone mixture into 4 small ramekin dishes. Scatter two-thirds of the raspberries in the dishes, then spoon in the melted chocolate and cream mixture.

3 Cover with the remaining mascarpone mixture and raspberries. Smooth the surface. Sprinkle with an even layer of caster sugar.

4 Preheat the grill to moderately hot and grill for 3–4 minutes, watching closely, until lightly caramelized. Chill for about 30 minutes until ready to serve.

Chocolate and Banana Creams

Muscovado sugar dissolves into cream and yogurt to make a lovely, treacly syrup. This simple dessert is great for both family meals and entertaining.

Serves: **4**

Preparation time: 10 minutes, plus chilling

Cooking time: 5 minutes

200 g/7 oz Cadbury's Dairy Milk chocolate, broken into pieces
150 ml/¼ pint double cream
2 ripe bananas
finely grated rind and juice of ½ lemon
200 g/7 oz Greek yogurt
40 g/1½ oz dark muscovado sugar
chocolate curls, to decorate (see page 8)

1 Melt the chocolate with 4 tablespoons of the cream, then stir gently until smooth. Mash the bananas by hand with the lemon juice. Stir in the yogurt.

2 Stir the remaining cream into the chocolate mixture. Divide one-third of the mixture among 4 serving glasses and sprinkle with a little of the sugar. Divide half the banana mixture among the glasses and sprinkle some sugar over the top. Repeat the layers, finishing with a chocolate layer.

3 Chill for at least 30 minutes until the sugar has dissolved. Decorate with chocolate curls before serving.

Red Fruit Pavlovas with Chocolate Sauce

These individual pavlovas should be crisp on the outside and marshmallowy inside. The chocolate sauce, which can be served either warm or cold, can be spooned over just before serving.

Serves: **8**

Preparation time: 20 minutes

Cooking time: 50–55 minutes

3 Cadbury's Flake
4 egg whites
200 g/7 oz caster sugar
1 teaspoon cornflour
1 teaspoon white wine vinegar
350 g/11½ oz strawberries or raspberries
150 ml/¼ pint double cream
SAUCE
200 g/7 oz Cadbury's Bournville chocolate, broken into pieces
4 tablespoons milk
3 tablespoons golden syrup
½ teaspoon vanilla essence
25 g/1 oz unsalted butter

1 Line a large baking sheet with nonstick paper. Coarsely crumble the Flake.

2 Whisk the egg whites in a large bowl until stiff. Gradually whisk in the sugar, 1 tablespoonful at a time, until the meringue is stiff and glossy. Stir in the cornflour, vinegar and two-thirds of the crumbled Flake. Divide the mixture into 8 mounds on the baking sheet, spreading each one to about 7 cm/3 inches in diameter and making a dip in the centre. Bake in a preheated oven, 140°C (275°F), Gas Mark 1, for 45–50 minutes until crisp. Leave to cool.

3 For the sauce, put the chocolate, milk, golden syrup and vanilla essence into a small heavy-based saucepan and heat gently, stirring frequently until the chocolate has melted. Stir in the butter. Continue stirring until the sauce is smooth, then pour it into a jug.

4 Slice the strawberries, if using. Whip the cream, fold in the fruit and spoon the mixture on to the meringues. Decorate with the remaining crumbled Flake and serve with the sauce.

Chocolate Lime Creams

A lime-flavoured syrup, whipped together with cream and grated chocolate, makes a creamy dessert that tastes both sweet and tangy. You can use plain or milk chocolate.

Serves: **4**

Preparation time: 5 minutes, plus chilling

Cooking time: 2 minutes

100 g/3½ oz Cadbury's Bournville
  chocolate or Cadbury's Dairy Milk
  chocolate
50 g/2 oz caster sugar
finely grated rind and juice of 2 limes
2 tablespoons water
300 ml/½ pint double cream

1 Coarsely grate the chocolate. Heat the sugar in a small saucepan with the lime rind and juice and the water until the sugar has dissolved. Cool slightly.
2 Put the lime syrup into a bowl with the cream and whisk until softly peaking. Reserve a little of the grated chocolate. Fold the remainder into the cream and spoon the mixture into serving glasses. Serve chilled, sprinkled with the reserved grated chocolate.

large cakes and teabreads

All the teatime favourites are here, from sponges and moist sticky cakes to teabreads marbled with plain or milk chocolate. There are some unusual flavour combinations, too. Ring the changes with chocolate cakes flavoured with orange, ginger, apples, coffee and walnuts, bananas and pecans, or even stout.

Really Moist Chocolate Slice

Plenty of almonds and butter give this moist cake a rich flavour. For an everyday version, dust the cake with icing sugar instead of filling and covering it with chocolate cream.

Serves: 12–14

Preparation time: 20 minutes

Cooking time: 45 minutes

250 g/8 oz Cadbury's Bournville chocolate, broken into pieces
250 g/8 oz unsalted butter, melted
5 eggs
50 g/2 oz light muscovado sugar
125 g/4 oz self-raising flour
75 g/3 oz ground almonds
CHOCOLATE CREAM
150 ml/¼ pint double cream
150 g/5 oz Cadbury's Bournville chocolate, chopped

1 Grease and line a 23 cm/9 inch square cake tin. Put the chocolate in a heatproof bowl, place over a pan of gently simmering water and leave until melted. Stir in the butter.

2 Beat together the eggs and sugar until slightly thickened. Sift the flour over the mixture, then add the almonds and chocolate mixture and fold in until evenly combined. Turn into the prepared tin and bake in a preheated oven, 160°C (325°F), Gas Mark 3, for about 35 minutes until just firm. Transfer to a wire rack to cool.

3 Meanwhile, make the chocolate cream. Heat the cream in a saucepan until almost boiling. Remove the pan from the heat and add the chocolate. Leave until the chocolate has melted, then stir until smooth. Transfer to a bowl and leave to cool until thickened.

4 Slice off the top of the cake if it has risen in the centre. Halve the cake horizontally and sandwich the halves with one-third of the chocolate cream. Spread the remainder over the top and sides of the cake, swirling it decoratively with a palette knife.

Chocolate Madeira Teabread

For added texture and flavour, this simple teabread is packed with chunky pieces of melt-in-the-mouth Cadbury's Dairy Milk chocolate.

Serves: **10**

Preparation time: 12 minutes

Cooking time: 1 hour 10 minutes

175 g/6 oz butter or margarine, softened
175 g/6 oz light muscovado sugar
3 eggs
2 tablespoons milk
200 g/7 oz self-raising flour
25 g/1 oz cocoa powder
200 g/7 oz Cadbury's Dairy Milk chocolate, chopped
cocoa powder, for dusting

1 Grease and line the base and long sides of a 1 kg/2 lb loaf tin. Cream the butter or margarine and sugar together in a bowl.

2 Add the eggs and milk, then sift the flour and cocoa powder into the bowl. Beat well until light and creamy. Stir in the chopped chocolate and turn the mixture into the prepared tin. Bake in a preheated oven, 180°C (350°F), Gas Mark 4, for 1 hour 10 minutes until just firm and a skewer inserted into the centre comes out clean.

3 Leave the teabread to cool in the tin for 10 minutes, then transfer to a wire rack to cool completely. Serve dusted with cocoa powder.

Orange-drizzled Chocolate Sponge

Once baked, this cake is generously drizzled with orange-flavoured syrup, which seeps into the sponge. Served warm and topped with thick yogurt or cream, it doubles as a simple pudding.

Serves: **8–10**

Preparation time: 20 minutes

Cooking time: 50–55 minutes

200 g/7 oz Cadbury's Bournville chocolate, broken into pieces
3 tablespoons milk
225 g/7½ oz self-raising flour
½ teaspoon bicarbonate of soda
125 g/4 oz unsalted butter, softened
150 g/5 oz caster sugar
2 eggs
200 g/7 oz thick Greek yogurt
SYRUP
200 g/7 oz caster sugar
150 ml/¼ pint water
grated rind and juice of 2 small oranges

1 Grease and line a 23 cm/9 inch springform cake tin. Put the chocolate and milk into a small saucepan and heat gently until the chocolate has melted.

2 Sift the flour and bicarbonate of soda into a bowl. Add the butter, sugar, eggs, yogurt and chocolate mixture and beat together until evenly combined. Turn into the prepared tin and bake in a preheated oven, 180°C (350°F), Gas Mark 4, for 45–50 minutes until just firm.

3 Meanwhile, for the syrup, heat the sugar and water in a small heavy-based saucepan until the sugar has dissolved. Boil for 3 minutes, then stir in the orange rind and juice and boil for 1 minute more.

4 Leave the cake to cool in the tin for 10 minutes, then pierce the top of the cake 5 or 6 times with a skewer. Spoon the syrup over the cake, allowing the syrup to trickle down the skewer holes. Serve warm or cold.

Frosted Chocolate Layer Cake

Serves: **12**

Preparation time: 20 minutes

Cooking time: 30 minutes

150 g/5 oz butter or margarine, softened
225 g/7½ oz caster sugar
2 eggs
150 g/5 oz Cadbury's Bournville chocolate, broken into pieces
200 ml/7 fl oz stout
50 g/2 oz cocoa powder
175 g/6 oz plain flour
½ teaspoon baking powder
1 teaspoon bicarbonate of soda
chocolate curls, to decorate (see page 8)

FROSTING

250 g/8 oz mascarpone cheese
200 g/7 oz icing sugar
4 teaspoons lemon juice

1 Grease and base-line 2 x 20 cm/8 inch round sandwich tins. Cream together the butter or margarine and sugar, then beat in the eggs. Put the chocolate in a heat-proof bowl with half the stout. Place over a pan of gently simmering water and leave until the chocolate has melted.
2 Beat the cocoa into the remaining stout, then stir the mixture into the melted chocolate. Sift together the flour, baking powder and soda. Fold the flour and chocolate mixtures alternately into the egg mixture. Divide between the tins and level the surfaces. Bake in a preheated oven, 180°C (350°F), Gas Mark 4, for about 25 minutes until just firm. Transfer to a wire rack and leave to cool.
3 For the frosting, beat the mascarpone in a bowl to soften. Add the icing sugar and lemon juice and beat until smooth. Sandwich the cakes together with one-third of the mixture, then spread the remaining frosting over the top. Decorate with plenty of chocolate curls.

Chocolate Marble Teabread

Spooning alternate layers of light and dark chocolate cake mixture into a loaf tin creates an interesting marbled look when the cake is sliced.

Serves: **8–10**

Preparation time: 10 minutes

Cooking time: 1¼ hours

100 g/3½ oz Cadbury's Bournville chocolate, broken into pieces
175 g/6 oz unsalted butter or margarine, softened
175 g/6 oz caster sugar
3 eggs
225 g/7½ oz self-raising flour
1 teaspoon baking powder
2 standard packets Cadbury Land Creamy-White Buttons
cocoa powder or icing sugar, for dusting

1 Grease the base and long sides of a 1 kg/2 lb loaf tin. Melt the plain chocolate.
2 Put the butter or margarine, sugar and eggs in a mixing bowl. Sift the flour and baking powder into the bowl. Beat until the mixture is smooth and creamy. Spoon half the mixture into a separate bowl.
3 Stir the melted chocolate into one half of the mixture and the Buttons into the other. Place alternate dessertspoons of the 2 mixtures in the prepared tin. Level the surface and bake in a preheated oven, 180°C (350°F), Gas Mark 4, for 1 hour 10 minutes or until just firm and a skewer inserted into the centre comes out clean.
4 Leave the teabread in the tin for 10 minutes, then transfer to a wire rack to cool. Serve dusted with cocoa powder or icing sugar.

Chocolate Ripple Teabread

In this simple recipe melted chocolate and butter are layered with the cake mixture so that they rise during cooking to give a decorative rippled effect.

Serves: **10**

Preparation time: 15 minutes

Cooking time: 1½ hours

200 g/7 oz Cadbury's Bournville chocolate, broken into pieces
200 g/7 oz unsalted butter or margarine, softened
1 teaspoon ground mixed spice
175 g/6 oz caster sugar
3 eggs
2 teaspoons vanilla essence
225 g/7½ oz self-raising flour
½ teaspoon baking powder
100 g/3½ oz Cadbury's Bournville chocolate, chopped, to decorate

1 Grease the base and long sides of a 1 kg/2 lb loaf tin. Put the chocolate in a heatproof bowl, place over a pan of gently simmering water and leave until melted. Stir in 25 g/1 oz of the butter or margarine and the spice.

2 Place the remaining butter or margarine, the sugar, eggs and vanilla essence in a bowl. Sift the flour and baking powder into the bowl and beat until light and fluffy. Spoon one-quarter of the mixture into the tin. Spread one-third of the chocolate mixture over the cake mixture. Repeat the layering of the cake mixture and chocolate sauce, finishing with a layer of cake mixture. Sprinkle with the chopped chocolate.

3 Bake in a preheated oven, 180°C (350°F), Gas Mark 4, for 1¼ hours or until risen and a skewer inserted into the centre of the teabread comes out clean. Leave in the tin for 10 minutes, then transfer to a wire rack to cool.

Sticky Chocolate Gingercake

Serves: **12**

Preparation time: 15 minutes

Cooking time: 55 minutes

75 g/3 oz stem ginger pieces, plus
 4–6 tablespoons syrup from the jar
125 g/4 oz black treacle
125 g/4 oz golden syrup
300 g/10 oz Cadbury's Bournville
 chocolate, broken into pieces
150 g/5 oz butter or margarine
350 g/11½ oz plain flour
1 teaspoon bicarbonate of soda
2 teaspoon ground ginger
2 eggs
50 g/2 oz Cadbury Land milk chocolate
 Buttons

1 Grease and line a deep 20 cm/8 inch square cake tin. Thinly slice the stem ginger. Put the treacle, golden syrup and chocolate in a heavy-based saucepan and heat very gently until the syrup starts to bubble. Remove from the heat and stir occasionally until the chocolate has melted. Stir in the butter or margarine.
2 Sift together the flour, bicarbonate of soda and ground ginger and add the mixture to the pan with the eggs and half the quantity of stem ginger slices. Stir until combined, then turn the mixture into the tin, spreading it into the corners.

3 Scatter the remaining ginger slices and the Buttons over the top and bake in a preheated oven, 160°C (325°F), Gas Mark 3, for 50 minutes or until firm to the touch. Drizzle the ginger syrup over the cake and leave to cool.

Chocolate Crumble Cake

Laden with chocolate and a crumbly, oaty topping, this gorgeous cake doubles as a dessert, particularly if you lavish it with cream.

Serves: **10**

Preparation time: 20 minutes

Cooking time: 50 minutes

300 g/10 oz Cadbury's Bournville
 chocolate
250 g/8 oz firm unsalted butter
400 g/13 oz plain flour
1 teaspoon baking powder
1 teaspoon ground cinnamon
125 g/4 oz caster sugar
1 egg
25 g/1 oz porridge oats
3 tablespoons demerara sugar

1 Grease a 20 cm/8 inch springform cake tin. Break 200 g/7 oz of the chocolate into pieces. Melt the chocolate in a heatproof bowl over a pan of gently simmering water. Add 25 g/1 oz of the butter and stir until smooth.

2 Put the flour, baking powder and cinnamon in a food processor. Add the remaining butter and blend until the mixture resembles coarse breadcrumbs. Blend in the caster sugar.
3 Reserve 250 g/8 oz of the crumble mixture. Add the egg to the remainder and mix to a firm paste. Press the paste into the base of the prepared tin. Spoon the melted chocolate mixture over the base to within 1 cm/½ inch of the edge.
4 Chop the remaining chocolate and mix it with the reserved crumble mixture, the oats and demerara sugar. Sprinkle it over the chocolate layer in the tin. Bake in a preheated oven, 180°C (350°F), Gas Mark 4, for 45 minutes or until golden.

Spiced Chocolate and Apple Slice

Softly baked apples make a sweet and tangy contrast to the sticky chocolate sponge in this delicious teatime slice.

Serves: **9**

Preparation time: 25 minutes

Cooking time: 45–50 minutes

175 g/6 oz butter or margarine, softened
175 g/6 oz caster sugar
3 eggs
150 g/5 oz plain flour
½ teaspoon baking powder
25 g/1 oz cocoa powder
1 teaspoon ground mixed spice
3 dessert apples
200 g/7 oz Cadbury's Bournville chocolate, chopped
100 g/3½ oz icing sugar
about 5 teaspoons cold water

1 Grease and base-line a 23 cm/9 inch square shallow baking tin. Beat together the butter or margarine, sugar, eggs, flour, baking powder, cocoa powder and spice.

2 Peel, core and chop 1 apple and add to the mixture with the chopped chocolate. Turn the mixture into the prepared tin and level the surface. Core and thinly slice the remaining apples. Arrange the slices in overlapping lines on top of the cake. Bake in a preheated oven, 180°C (350°F), Gas Mark 4, for 45–50 minutes until the cake is just firm in the centre.

3 Mix the icing sugar with the water to make a thin icing. Transfer the cake to a wire rack and spoon the icing over the top. Leave to cool.

variation
Ripe pears make an equally good alternative to the apples.

Chocolate Sponge Sandwich

For many chocolate lovers a simple chocolate sponge is hard to beat, particularly if it's chocolate-chip-flavoured. For a variation that will keep longer, sandwich the cake with chocolate buttercream instead of fresh cream.

Serves: **10–12**

Preparation time: 20 minutes

Cooking time: 25 minutes

225 g/7½ oz margarine, softened
225 g/7½ oz caster sugar
4 eggs
200 g/7 oz self-raising flour
25 g/1 oz cocoa powder
1½ teaspoons baking powder
150 g/5 oz Cadbury's Dairy Milk chocolate, chopped
TO FINISH
150 ml/¼ pint double cream
75 g/3 oz icing sugar
3 tablespoons cocoa powder

1 Grease and base-line 2 x 20 cm/8 inch sandwich tins. Put the margarine, sugar and eggs in a bowl. Sift the flour, cocoa powder and baking powder into the bowl, then beat well until creamy.

2 Stir in the chocolate. Divide the mixture between the tins and level the surfaces. Bake in a preheated oven, 180°C (350°F), Gas Mark 4, for 25 minutes or until risen and just firm to the touch in the centre. Transfer to a wire rack to cool.

3 Whip the cream and use it to sandwich the cakes together. Sift the icing sugar and cocoa powder into a bowl and add enough water to make an icing the consistency of pouring cream. Spoon the icing over the top and side of the cake.

Flake, Fruit and Nut Cake

A really easy fruit cake that provides plenty of servings. Chunks of chopped Cadbury's Flake, Cadbury's Bournville chocolate, dried fruit and nuts give it a lovely crumbly texture.

Serves: **12**

Preparation time: 15 minutes

Cooking time: about 2 hours

3 Cadbury's Flake
225 g/7½ oz butter or margarine, softened
225 g/7½ oz caster sugar
275 g/9 oz self-raising flour
25 g/1 oz cocoa powder
4 eggs
150 g/5 oz hazelnuts, roughly chopped
200 g/7 oz Cadbury's Bournville chocolate, chopped
225 g/7½ oz raisins
cocoa powder or icing sugar, for dusting

1 Grease and line a 20 cm/8 inch round or 18 cm/7 inch square cake tin. Cut all the Flake into 1.5 cm/¾ inch pieces. Cream together the butter or margarine and sugar.

2 Add the flour, cocoa powder and eggs to the bowl and beat until smooth. Reserve half of the pieces of Flake and 50 g/2 oz of the hazelnuts and plain chocolate. Fold the remainder into the cake mixture with the raisins.

3 Turn into the prepared tin and scatter with the reserved chocolate and nuts. Bake in a preheated oven, 150°C (300°F), Gas Mark 2, for about 2 hours or until a skewer inserted into the centre comes out clean. Leave to cool in the tin. Serve lightly dusted with cocoa powder or icing sugar.

Chocolate Mousse Cake

Rather like a soufflé, this moist cake rises during cooking, then deflates as it cools, developing a lovely mousse-like texture. It's good served with a little cream, or scattered with sugared raspberries or blueberries.

Serves: **8**

Preparation time: 20 minutes

Cooking time: 35 minutes

200 g/7 oz Cadbury's Bournville chocolate, broken into pieces
2 tablespoons brandy
125 g/4 oz unsalted butter, melted
5 eggs, separated
125 g/4 oz caster sugar

1 Grease and line a 23 cm/9 inch springform cake tin. Melt the chocolate with the brandy, then stir in the butter until smooth.
2 Put the egg yolks in a bowl with 75 g/3 oz of the sugar and whisk until pale and thickened. Stir in the chocolate mixture.

3 Whisk the egg whites in a separate bowl until stiff. Gradually whisk in the remaining sugar. Using a large metal spoon, fold the egg whites into the chocolate mixture until just combined. Turn into the prepared tin and bake in a preheated oven, 160°C (325°F), Gas Mark 3, for 35 minutes or until well risen and the surface is beginning to crack. Leave to cool in the tin, then carefully transfer to a serving plate.

variation

As an interesting flavour variation, try adding 1 teaspoon of ground mixed spice to the chocolate mixture before folding in the egg whites.

Chocolate, Banana and Pecan Cake

A great cake for using up bananas that have been left in the fruitbowl for too long and are a bit over-ripe.

Serves: **8–10**

Preparation time: 20 minutes

Cooking time: 50–60 minutes

2 large bananas
250 g/8 oz self-raising flour
1 teaspoon baking powder
150 g/5 oz butter or margarine, softened
150 g/5 oz caster sugar
3 eggs
100 g/3½ oz pecan nuts, roughly chopped
200 g/7 oz Cadbury's Dairy Milk chocolate, chopped

1 Grease and line the base and long sides of a 1 kg/2 lb loaf tin. Mash the bananas with a fork.
2 Sift the flour and baking powder into a bowl. Add the butter or margarine, sugar and eggs and beat well until smooth. Beat in the bananas, half the pecan nuts and 150 g/5 oz of the chocolate.
3 Turn the mixture into the prepared tin and level the surface. Scatter the reserved nuts and chocolate over the top. Bake in a preheated oven, 180°C (350°F), Gas Mark 4, for 50–60 minutes or until risen and a skewer inserted into the centre comes out clean. Leave to cool in the tin.

Mocha and Walnut Sponge

Anyone who likes coffee and walnut cake will enjoy this variation on the theme, with its chocolate bonus. For a less rich version, serve without the cream topping.

Serves: **12**

Preparation time: 15 minutes

Cooking time: 50 minutes

4 teaspoons instant coffee granules
2 tablespoons hot water
200 g/7 oz Cadbury's Bournville chocolate, broken into pieces
225 g/7½ oz butter or margarine, softened
225 g/7½ oz caster sugar
5 eggs
125 g/4 oz ground almonds
150 g/5 oz plain flour
100 g/3½ oz walnut pieces
TO FINISH
150 ml/¼ pint strong black coffee
2 tablespoons caster sugar
150 ml/¼ pint double cream
cocoa powder, for dusting

1 Grease a 23 cm/9 inch springform cake tin. Dissolve the coffee granules in the hot water. Put the chocolate in a heatproof bowl with the coffee and melt the chocolate over a pan of gently simmering water.

2 Beat together the butter or margarine, sugar, eggs, almonds and flour until creamy. Stir in the melted chocolate and all but 3 tablespoons of the walnuts. Turn the mixture into the prepared tin and level the surface. Bake in a preheated oven, 180°C (350°F), Gas Mark 4, for 45 minutes or until just firm. Leave in the tin.

3 Put the coffee and sugar in a small saucepan and heat gently until the sugar dissolves. Bring to the boil and boil for 2 minutes until the mixture is syrupy. Leave to cool slightly, then drizzle the syrup over the cake. Leave to cool.

4 Whip the cream until softly peaking. Transfer the cake to a serving plate and spread the cream over it. Dust with cocoa powder and scatter the reserved walnuts over the top.

Chocolate Fudge Ring

This classic chocolate fudge cake is baked in a ring tin, then layered and covered with chocolate fudge icing. The finished cake, or portions of it, can be frozen for another time, so you can eliminate the risk of over-indulgence.

Serves: 12

Preparation time: 20 minutes

Cooking time: 40 minutes

175 g/6 oz self-raising flour
50 g/2 oz cocoa powder
2 teaspoons baking powder
175 g/6 oz caster sugar
175 g/6 oz butter or margarine, softened
4 eggs
2 teaspoons vanilla essence
4 tablespoons milk
walnut halves, to decorate
FUDGE ICING
300 g/10 oz Cadbury's Bournville chocolate, broken into pieces
4 tablespoons milk
50 g/2 oz unsalted butter, softened
225 g/7½ oz icing sugar, plus extra for dusting

1 Grease and line the base of a 1.8 litre/3 pint ring cake tin. Sift the flour, cocoa and baking powder into a bowl. Add the sugar, butter or margarine, eggs, vanilla essence and milk and beat with an electric whisk for 1–2 minutes (or 3 minutes with a wooden spoon) until evenly combined.

2 Turn the mixture into the prepared tin and level the surface. Bake in a preheated oven, 180°C (350°F), Gas Mark 4, for 35 minutes or until just firm to the touch. Use a palette knife to loosen the cake from the side of the tin, then invert the cake on to a wire rack and leave to cool.

3 For the fudge icing, put the chocolate in a heavy-based saucepan with the milk . Heat gently until the chocolate has melted, stirring frequently. Stir in the butter. Beat in the icing sugar and leave the mixture to cool slightly.

4 Split the cake horizontally into three layers. Beat the icing again until it has a slightly fudge-like texture. Use a little icing to sandwich the layers together. Spread the remaining icing over the top and sides of the cake, swirling it with a palette knife. Decorate with the walnut halves and dust with icing sugar.

small cakes

They say small is beautiful, and that certainly applies to this selection of tempting little mouthfuls. Indulge your family and friends with irresistible homemade chocolate éclairs, Viennese whirls, double chocolate brownies and triple chocolate muffins or a shortbread that belongs in the millionaire league.

Chocolate Cherry Patties

These tempting little cakes won't last long in the cake tin – they're irresistible. Canned apricots, thickly sliced, make a good alternative to the cherries.

Makes: **12**

Preparation time: 15 minutes

Cooking time: 25 minutes

175 g/6 oz butter or margarine
100 g/3½ oz Cadbury's Bournville
  chocolate
425 g/14 oz can pitted black or red
  cherries in syrup
150 g/5 oz ground almonds
150 g/5 oz caster sugar
40 g/1½ oz plain flour
4 egg whites
icing sugar, for dusting

1 Lightly grease a 12-section muffin tin. Melt the butter or margarine and leave to cool slightly. Coarsely grate the chocolate. Thoroughly drain the cherries.
2 Mix together the almonds, sugar and flour in a bowl. Add the egg whites, melted butter and chocolate and mix until evenly combined. Divide the mixture among the sections of the tin.
3 Arrange the cherries on top of the patties and bake in a preheated oven, 200°C (400°F), Gas Mark 6, for about 20 minutes until risen, golden and just firm in the centre. Leave in the tin for 10 minutes, then transfer to a wire rack to cool. Serve lightly dusted with icing sugar.

Chocolate Frangipane Brioches

Individual brioches, slightly hollowed out and filled with chocolate and almond paste make an instant treat. Served warmed through, they're very good for breakfast.

Makes: **4**

Preparation time: 10 minutes

Cooking time: 5–8 minutes

4 individual brioche
75 g/3 oz almond paste
100 g/3½ oz Cadbury's Bournville chocolate or Cadbury's Dairy Milk chocolate, chopped
icing sugar, for dusting

1 Slice the top off each brioche and reserve for use as lids, then roughly scoop out the centre of each brioche, leaving a case about 1 cm/½ inch thick.
2 Chop the almond paste and divide it among the brioches with the chocolate. Put the lids on top and bake in a preheated oven, 180°C (350°F), Gas Mark 4, for 5–8 minutes until warm through, but not too hot. (The chocolate should be slightly melted, but not too hot to eat.) Serve dusted with icing sugar.

Chocolate Whirls

A chocolate version of buttery little Viennese whirls. These are set in little paper cake cases and filled with melted chocolate after baking.

Makes: **12**

Preparation time: 15 minutes

Cooking time: 25 minutes

200 g/7 oz unsalted butter, softened
100 g/3½ oz caster sugar
200 g/7 oz plain flour
½ teaspoon baking powder
25 g/1 oz cocoa powder
2 teaspoons milk
100 g/3½ oz Cadbury's Bournville chocolate, broken into pieces

1 Line a 12-section tartlet tin with paper cake cases.
2 Beat together the butter and sugar until pale and creamy. Sift the flour, baking powder and cocoa powder into the bowl, add the milk and beat well to make a smooth paste.
3 Spoon the mixture into a piping bag fitted with a large star nozzle and pipe swirls into the cases, leaving a large cavity in the centre. Bake in a preheated oven, 190°C (375°F), Gas Mark 5, for 15–20 minutes or until slightly risen. Press a whole in the centre of each whirl. Leave to cool in the tin.
4 To decorate, melt the chocolate and spoon a little into the centre of each whirl. Leave to set slightly before serving.

variation
If you don't have a piping bag and a large star nozzle, simply spoon the mixture into the paper cases, making a cavity in the centre of each chocolate whirl. The cakes will look more irregular, but still appealing.

Triple Chocolate Muffins

To enjoy the light, airy texture of muffins, eat them on the day they're made or, if stored for a day or two, warm them through a little before serving. In this recipe, Cadbury's Creamy White Buttons are folded into the mixture, but you can use 75 g/3 oz chopped Cadbury's Dairy Milk chocolate instead.

Makes: **12**

Preparation time: 15 minutes

Cooking time: 25–30 minutes

300 g/10 oz Cadbury's Bournville chocolate, chopped
50 g/2 oz unsalted butter, melted
375 g/12 oz self-raising flour
1 tablespoon baking powder
50 g/2 oz cocoa powder
100 g/3½ oz caster sugar
1 egg
350 ml/12 fl oz milk
2 standard packets Cadbury Land Creamy-White Buttons

1 Line a 12-section deep bun tin or muffin tin with paper muffin cases. Melt 175 g/6 oz of the plain chocolate, then stir in the melted butter.

2 Sift the flour, baking powder and cocoa powder into a bowl. Stir in the sugar. Beat together the egg and milk and slowly beat this mixture into the melted chocolate.

3 Add the liquid mixture to the dry ingredients, then the remaining chopped chocolate and the Buttons.

4 Using a large metal spoon, fold the ingredients together until only just combined. Divide the mixture among the paper cases. Bake in a preheated oven, 200°C (400°F), Gas Mark 6, for 20–25 minutes until well risen and just firm. Serve the muffins warm or cold.

Millionaire's Shortbread

These chocolate treats combine buttery shortbread with gooey caramel and a thick layer of pure chocolate – they're out of this world.

Makes: **12**

Preparation time: 20 minutes, plus setting

Cooking time: 35 minutes

75 g/3 oz plain flour
50 g/2 oz unsalted butter
25 g/1 oz caster sugar
CARAMEL
397 g/14 oz can condensed milk
50 g/2 oz unsalted butter
50 g/2 oz caster sugar
TO FINISH
200 g/7 oz Cadbury's Bournville chocolate, broken into pieces
25 g/1 oz Cadbury's Dairy Milk chocolate, broken into pieces

1 Lightly grease an 18 cm/7 inch square loose-based cake tin. Put the flour and butter in a food processor and blend until the mixture resembles fine breadcrumbs. Add the sugar and mix to a dough.

2 Press the mixture into the prepared tin, packing it down into an even layer. Bake in a preheated oven, 180°C (350°F), Gas Mark 4, for 20 minutes or until pale golden. Leave to cool.

3 For the caramel, put the condensed milk, butter and sugar in a heavy-based saucepan and heat gently until the sugar dissolves. Bring to the boil, reduce the heat and simmer very gently for about 5 minutes until the mixture is thickened and pale golden in colour. Pour over the shortbread and leave to set for 2–3 hours.

4 Melt the plain and milk chocolate separately. Pour the plain chocolate over the caramel. Using a teaspoon, drizzle the milk chocolate over the plain chocolate. Swirl a cocktail stick through the two chocolates to marble them slightly. Leave to set. Serve cut into squares.

Chocolate, Orange and Oatmeal Muffins

A recipe for chocolate muffins, with chunky pieces of Cadbury's Dairy Milk chocolate and an oatmeal texture.

Makes: **9–10**

Preparation time: 10 minutes

Cooking time: 15–20 minutes

225 g/7½ oz plain flour
2 teaspoons baking powder
finely grated rind of 1 orange
50 g/2 oz medium oatmeal
75 g/3 oz light muscovado sugar
200 g/7 oz Greek yogurt
4 tablespoons sunflower or vegetable oil
150 ml/¼ pint milk
1 egg
200 g/7 oz Cadbury's Dairy Milk chocolate, chopped
oatmeal, for sprinkling

1 Line a 10-section deep bun tin or muffin tin with paper muffin cases. Sift the flour and baking powder into a bowl. Stir in the orange rind, oatmeal and sugar.
2 Beat the yogurt with the oil, milk and egg and add to the bowl of dry ingredients with the chopped chocolate. Using a large metal spoon, carefully fold the ingredients together until only just combined, adding a little extra milk if the mixture seems dry.
3 Divide the mixture among the paper cases and sprinkle some extra oatmeal over the top. Bake the muffins in a preheated oven, 200°C (400°F), Gas Mark 6, for 15–20 minutes until risen and just firm. Serve warm or cold.

variation
You can make 'mini' muffins by filling ordinary paper cake cases instead of the traditional muffin ones. Reduce the cooking time by about 5 minutes.

Fudge-frosted Cup Cakes

These little chocolate sponges, topped with a thick layer of chocolate fudge icing, make an irresistible treat.

Makes: **18**

Preparation time: 15 minutes

Cooking time: 20–23 minutes

125 g/4 oz unsalted butter or margarine, softened
125 g/4 oz caster sugar
2 eggs
75 g/3 oz self-raising flour
¼ teaspoon baking powder
40 g/1½ oz cocoa powder
ICING
150 g/5 oz Cadbury's Dairy Milk chocolate, broken into pieces
3 tablespoons milk
75 g/3 oz unsalted butter or margarine
125 g/4 oz icing sugar

1 Line 18 sections of deep bun tins or muffin tins with paper cake cases. (Bake in batches if necessary.) Put the butter or margarine, sugar, eggs, flour, baking powder and cocoa powder in a bowl and beat well until smooth and creamy.

2 Divide the mixture among the paper cases, filling no more than two-thirds full. Bake in a preheated oven, 190°C (375°F), Gas Mark 5, for 15–18 minutes or until risen and just firm. Leave to cool.

3 For the icing, put the chocolate and milk in a small heavy-based saucepan. Heat very gently, stirring frequently, until the chocolate has melted, then stir in the butter or margarine. Remove from the heat and stir in the icing sugar until smooth. While still hot, spoon the icing over the cakes and leave to set.

Soft-centre Teacakes

These simple little teacakes hide a pocket of chocolate in the centre.

Makes: **12**

Preparation time: 5 minutes

Cooking time: 20–25 minutes

75 g/3 oz Cadbury's Bournville chocolate or Cadbury's Dairy Milk chocolate, broken into pieces
140 g/4½ oz unsalted butter or margarine, softened
125 g/4 oz caster sugar
2 eggs
125 g/4 oz self-raising flour
¼ teaspoon baking powder
1 teaspoon vanilla essence
icing sugar, for dusting

1 Line a 12-section tartlet tin with paper cases. Melt the chocolate, then stir in 15 g/½ oz of the butter or margarine. Stir until smooth.

2 Put the remaining butter, the sugar, eggs, flour, baking powder and vanilla essence into a bowl and beat until smooth. Divide about two-thirds of the mixture among the paper cases, making a slight indentation in the centre of each portion with the back of a teaspoon.

3 Spoon the chocolate sauce into the centres, then cover with the remaining cake mixture. Bake in a preheated oven, 180°C (350°F), Gas Mark 4, for 15–20 minutes until risen and just firm. Leave to cool, then dust with icing sugar.

variation

For a double chocolate version, use 15 g/½ oz cocoa powder instead of 15 g/½ oz of the flour. Once baked, dust the tops with cocoa powder.

Chocolate Eclairs

For some chocoholics, the combination of choux pastry filled with whipped cream and covered with chocolate is an unbeatable luxury, and homemade éclairs are definitely the best. The pastry can be made ahead and stored in an airtight container for 2–3 days or frozen. Re-crisp the pastry cases in a moderate oven for a few minutes before filling.

Makes: **12–14**

Preparation time: 20 minutes, plus cooling

Cooking time: 40–45 minutes

60 g/2½ oz plain flour
50 g/2 oz unsalted butter
150 ml/¼ pint water
2 eggs, beaten
TO FINISH
300 ml/½ pint double cream
2 teaspoons icing sugar
1 teaspoon vanilla essence
150 g/5 oz Cadbury's Bournville chocolate, broken into pieces
15 g/½ oz unsalted butter

1 Lightly grease a large baking sheet and sprinkle it with water. Sift the flour on to a piece of paper.
2 Put the butter and water in a saucepan and heat gently until the butter melts. Bring to the boil and remove from the heat. Tip in the flour and beat until the mixture forms a ball which comes away from the side of the pan. Leave to cool for 2 minutes.
3 Gradually beat the eggs into the dough a little at a time, until the pastry is smooth and glossy. Put the pastry in a large piping bag fitted with a 1 cm/½ inch plain nozzle. Pipe 12–14 x 7 cm/3 inch fingers of dough on to the baking sheet, spacing them about 5 cm/2 inches apart. Bake in a preheated oven, 200°C (400°F), Gas Mark 6, for 30–35 minutes until well risen and crisp.
4 Make a slit down the side of each pastry and return them to the oven for a further 3 minutes to dry out. Transfer to a wire rack and leave to cool.
5 Whip the cream with the icing sugar and vanilla essence until the mixture just begins to hold its shape. Spoon a little of the mixture into each of the éclairs.
6 For the topping, melt the chocolate, then stir in the butter until smooth. Using a teaspoon, drizzle the chocolate over the éclairs. Leave to set.

variation
If you haven't got a large piping bag and nozzle, use a teaspoon to shape similar-sized lengths of dough on the baking sheet. Alternatively, spoon little mounds of pastry to make small choux buns.

Very Chunky Chocolate Brownies

Chocolate brownies are an all-time favourite. Gooey, sugary and rich, the results are well worth the quantity of chocolate used. Any other nuts can be substituted for the walnuts, or they can be left out altogether.

Makes: **18**

Preparation time: 20 minutes

Cooking time: 45 minutes

200 g/7 oz Cadbury's Dairy Milk chocolate
300 g/10 oz Cadbury's Bournville chocolate, broken into pieces
225 g/7½ oz unsalted butter, softened
3 eggs
225 g/7½ oz light muscovado sugar
75 g/3 oz self-raising flour
175 g/6 oz walnuts, broken

1 Grease and line a 28 x 20 cm/ 11 x 8 inch shallow baking tin. Roughly chop the milk chocolate. Melt the plain chocolate, then stir in the butter.

2 Beat together the eggs and sugar, then beat in the melted plain chocolate mixture. Stir in the flour, walnuts and milk chocolate. Turn the mixture into the prepared tin and level the surface bake in a preheated oven, 190°C (375°F), Gas Mark 5, for about 40 minutes until the centre feels just firm on the crust but soft underneath. Take care not to overcook the brownies will be dry. Leave to cool in the tin.

3 When cool, turn out the cake and cut it into 18 squares.

biscuits and cookies

From Italian-style walnut biscotti to American-style double chocolate cookies, and from sophisticated little biscuits flavoured with mulled wine and spices to jolly gingerbread people, this chapter is filled with delectable recipes for all ages and tastes. Nibble them with morning coffee or at teatime or as an accompaniment to ice creams and chilled desserts.

Chocolate Walnut Biscotti

There's an interesting technique for making these Italian-style biscuits. The dough is part-baked, then sliced and baked again to achieve the familiar crisp shapes.

Makes: **20**

Preparation time: 15 minutes

Cooking time: 40 minutes

200 g/7 oz Cadbury's Bournville chocolate,
  broken into pieces
25 g/1 oz unsalted butter, softened
200 g/7 oz self-raising flour
1½ teaspoons baking powder
100 g/3½ oz light muscovado sugar
50 g/2 oz ground semolina or polenta
finely grated rind of ½ orange
1 egg
1 teaspoon vanilla essence
100 g/3½ oz broken walnuts
icing sugar, for dusting

1 Lightly grease a large baking sheet. Melt the chocolate, then stir in the butter.
2 Sift the flour and baking powder into a bowl. Add the sugar, semolina or polenta, orange rind, egg, vanilla essence and walnuts. Add the melted chocolate and butter and mix to form a dough. If the mixture feels dry, add 1 tablespoon water.
3 Turn the dough out on to a lightly floured surface and divide it in half. Shape each half into a sausage, about 28 cm/11 inches long. Transfer each sausage to the prepared baking sheet and flatten to about 1.5 cm/¾ inch thick. Bake in a preheated oven, 160°C (325°F), Gas Mark 3, for 25 minutes or until risen and firm.
4 Leave to cool, then diagonally slice each slab into 1.5 cm/¾ inch thick biscuits. Return the biscuits to the baking sheet, spacing them slightly apart, and bake for a further 10 minutes until crisp. Leave to cool, then dust with icing sugar.

variation
Roughly chopped hazelnuts, almonds or Brazil nuts are all possible alternatives to walnuts in this recipe.

Chocolate Florentines

This combination of rich Cadbury's Bournville chocolate and dried fruit and nuts is a classic, special occasion biscuit.

Makes: **12–14**

Preparation time: 12 minutes

Cooking time: 25–35 minutes

25 g/1 oz glacé cherries
60 g/2½ oz unsalted butter
50 g/2 oz caster sugar
2 tablespoons double cream
25 g/1 oz raisins or sultanas
25 g/1 oz mixed candied peel
50 g/2 oz flaked almonds
2 tablespoons plain flour
150 g/5 oz Cadbury's Bournville chocolate, broken into pieces

1 Lightly grease a large baking sheet, preferably nonstick. Roughly chop the cherries.
2 Melt the butter in a small saucepan. Stir in the sugar and heat until bubbling. Remove from the heat and stir in the cream, dried fruit, almonds, flour and glacé cherries.

3 Place teaspoonfuls of the mixture, spaced well apart, on the baking sheet. (You'll probably need to bake them in at least 2 batches.) Bake in a preheated oven, 180°C (350°F), Gas Mark 4, for about 8 minutes until the mixture has spread. Immediately, use an oiled plain biscuit cutter to push in the edge of each biscuit to make neat rounds. Bake for a further 2 minutes, then transfer the Florentines to a sheet of nonstick baking parchment to cool. Bake the remaining mixture in the same way.
4 Melt the chocolate. Using a palette knife, spread the underside of each biscuit with plenty of chocolate and leave to set on a clean sheet of paper.

Chocolate Chip Flapjacks

Flapjacks are just about the easiest thing you can bake. Chunks of finely chopped Cadbury's Dairy Milk make this version particularly good, but make sure you let the mixture cool before adding the chocolate, or it will melt.

Makes: **about 24**

Preparation time: 15 minutes

Cooking time: 25–30 minutes

225 g/7½ oz unsalted butter or margarine
225 g/7½ oz light muscovado sugar
175 g/6 oz golden syrup
300 g/10 oz Cadbury's Dairy Milk chocolate, chopped
400 g/13 oz porridge oats

1 Lightly grease a 28 x 20 cm/11 x 8 inch shallow baking tin. Melt the butter or margarine with the sugar and golden syrup and leave to cool completely.
2 Mix together the chocolate and oats in a bowl. Add the syrup mixture and stir until evenly combined. Turn the mixture into the prepared tin and level the surface.
3 Bake in a preheated oven, 180°C (350°F), Gas Mark 4, for 20–25 minutes until just beginning to colour around the edges. Leave in the tin until almost cold, then transfer to a board and cut into fingers. Store in an airtight container.

Mulled Wine Biscuits

Makes: **about 25**

Preparation time: 15 minutes

Cooking time: 25–30 minutes

140 g/4½ oz raisins
75 g/3 oz dried cranberries
150 ml/¼ pint red wine
100 g/3½ oz redcurrant jelly
1 teaspoon ground cinnamon
¼ teaspoon ground cloves
good pinch of chilli powder
50 g/2 oz walnuts
50 g/2 oz whole blanched almonds
100 g/3½ oz Cadbury's Bournville
   chocolate
75 g/3 oz self-raising flour
finely grated rind of 1 orange
50 g/2 oz unsalted butter, melted
1 egg
icing sugar, for dusting

1 Put the raisins and cranberries in a small heavy-based saucepan with the wine, jelly and spices. Heat until the jelly dissolves, then bring to the boil and boil for 2–3 minutes until the syrup is reduced by about half. Leave to cool.

2 Lightly grease a large baking sheet. Chop the nuts and chocolate. Mix in a bowl with the flour, orange rind, melted butter, egg and fruit mixture to make a paste. Place teaspoonfuls of the mixture, spaced slightly apart, on the prepared baking sheet.

3 Bake in a preheated oven, 180°C (350°F), Gas Mark 4, for about 20 minutes until the biscuits have spread slightly. Leave them on the baking sheet for 3 minutes, then transfer to a wire rack to cool. Dust generously with icing sugar. Store in an airtight container for up to 1 week.

Chocolate and Almond Shortbreads

Dress up homemade, buttery shortbread biscuits with a thick coating of rich dark chocolate and a scattering of flaked almonds.

Makes: **20**

Preparation time: 15 minutes, plus chilling

Cooking time: 25–30 minutes

150 g/5 oz plain flour
25 g/1 oz cornflour
125 g/4 oz firm unsalted butter
50 g/2 oz caster sugar
TO DECORATE
150 g/5 oz Cadbury's Bournville chocolate,
   broken into pieces
25 g/1 oz flaked or slivered almonds,
   lightly toasted

1 Put the flour and cornflour in a food processor. Add the butter, cut into small pieces, and blend until beginning to bind together. Add the sugar and mix to a dough. Turn out on to a lightly floured surface and shape the dough into a thick sausage, 15 cm/6 inches long. Wrap in clingfilm and chill for 30 minutes.

2 Lightly grease a large baking sheet. Using a sharp knife, cut the shortbread crossways into 20 x 5 mm/¼ inch thick slices and transfer to the baking sheet. Bake in a preheated oven, 160°C (325°F), Gas Mark 3, for 20–25 minutes until beginning to darken around the edges. Leave for 2 minutes, then transfer to a wire rack to cool.

3 Melt the chocolate. Place a sheet of paper under the wire rack to catch any drips, then spoon the melted chocolate over the biscuits. Scatter the almonds over each one as you finish coating it. Leave to set.

Chocolate Cigars

Rather like brandy snaps, these delicate biscuits are wrapped around spoon handles to achieve their cigar shape. Serve with coffee or as an elegant accompaniment to creamy desserts. If the biscuits set on the baking sheets before you've had time to shape them, simply pop them back in the oven for a few moments to soften.

Makes: **16**

Preparation time: 20 minutes, plus setting

Cooking time: 4 minutes each batch

1 egg white
50 g/2 oz caster sugar
2 tablespoons plain flour
1 tablespoon cocoa powder
2 tablespoons double cream
25 g/1 oz unsalted butter, melted
150 g/5 oz Cadbury's Bournville chocolate, broken into pieces

1 Line 4 baking sheets with nonstick baking parchment.

2 Whisk the egg white and sugar together until blended. Sift the flour and cocoa powder into the bowl. Stir in the cream and butter.

3 Place 4 dessertspoons of the mixture, spaced well apart, on one of the prepared baking sheets and spread lightly with the back of a spoon. Bake in a preheated oven 220°C (425°F), Gas Mark 7, for 4 minutes until the biscuits have spread and the edges are beginning to darken.

4 Remove from the oven and leave for 30 seconds. Using a palette knife, lift each biscuit from the paper and wrap them around the handles of wooden spoons until set into shape. Carefully twist the biscuits off the spoons and transfer them to a wire rack. Repeat with the remaining mixture on the remaining baking sheets.

5 Melt the chocolate and dip one side of each biscuit into it, letting the excess chocolate fall back into the bowl. Leave the biscuits on a sheet of greaseproof paper until they are set. Store in an airtight container.

Button Cookies

These miniature cookies are packed with Cadbury Land Creamy-White Buttons, giving them a lovely smooth flavour.

Makes: **about 25**

Preparation time: 10 minutes

Cooking time: 12–15 minutes

4 standard packets Cadbury Land Creamy-White Buttons
175 g/6 oz self-raising flour
75 g/3 oz firm unsalted butter
60 g/2½ oz light muscovado sugar
1 egg
1 teaspoon vanilla essence
icing sugar, for dusting

1 Lightly grease a large baking sheet. Using your fingers, break up the Buttons slightly by crushing them while still in their packets.

2 Put the flour in a food processor. Add the butter, cut into small pieces and blend until the dough is only just beginning to hold together.

3 Turn into a bowl and add the sugar, egg and vanilla essence. Reserve half a packet of the Buttons. Stir the remainder into the cookie mixture to make a thick, crumbly paste. Place teaspoonfuls of the mixture on the prepared baking sheet, spacing them slightly apart. Press the reserved Button pieces into the cookies. Bake in a preheated oven, 160°C (325°F), Gas Mark 3, for 12–15 minutes until turning pale golden.

4 Leave the cookies on the baking sheet for 2 minutes, then transfer to a wire rack to cool. Serve dusted with icing sugar.

Double Chocolate Cookies

These chunky, American-style oat cookies are packed full of chopped chocolate.

Makes: **about 16**

Preparation time: 10 minutes

Cooking time: 15 minutes

125 g/4 oz unsalted butter, softened
125 g/4 oz light muscovado sugar
1 egg
150 g/5 oz porridge oats
125 g/4 oz self-raising flour
100 g/3½ oz Cadbury's Bournville chocolate, chopped
100 g/3½ oz Cadbury's Dairy Milk chocolate, chopped

1 Lightly grease 2 baking sheets. In a large bowl, beat together the butter and sugar until creamy. Stir in the egg and oats.

2 Sift the flour into the bowl, then fold it in with the plain and milk chocolate. Place teaspoonfuls of the mixture on the prepared baking sheets and flatten them slightly using the back of the spoon.

3 Bake in a preheated oven, 180°C (350°F), Gas Mark 4, for 15 minutes or until slightly risen and pale golden. Leave the cookies on the baking sheets for 2 minutes, then transfer to a wire rack to cool. Store in an airtight container.

Chocolate Gingerbread People

There is a homely appeal about baking a batch of gingerbread people. Their simple, chubby shapes will be appreciated by young and old alike, especially as they have chocolate clothes.

Makes: **10–20, depending on size**

Preparation time: 20 minutes, plus setting

Cooking time: 30 minutes

300 g/10 oz plain flour
25 g/1 oz cocoa powder
2 teaspoons ground ginger
1 teaspoon bicarbonate of soda
125 g/4 oz unsalted butter or margarine
175 g/6 oz caster sugar
4 teaspoons golden syrup or black treacle
1 egg
50 g/2 oz Cadbury's Dairy Milk chocolate, broken into pieces
50 g/2 oz Cadbury's Bournville chocolate, broken into pieces

1 Lightly grease 2 baking sheets. Sift the flour, cocoa powder, ginger and bicarbonate of soda into a bowl. Cut the butter or margarine into small pieces and rub in using your fingertips until the mixture resembles breadcrumbs.

2 Add the sugar, syrup or treacle and egg and mix to form a firm dough. Knead until smooth. Roll out half the mixture on a lightly floured surface and cut out shapes, using a gingerbread cutter. Transfer to a baking sheet and bake in a preheated oven, 190°C (375°F), Gas Mark 5, for about 15 minutes until just beginning to darken around the edges. Repeat with the remaining dough. Leave the batches on the baking sheets for 3 minutes, then transfer to a wire rack to cool.

3 Melt the milk chocolate and plain chocolate separately. Use the chocolate to decorate the biscuits, spooning on 'clothes' with a teaspoon, and piping features and buttons using a piping bag. Leave to set.

Palmier Twists

These attractive biscuits are not too rich, so they go well with creamy desserts and ice cream. They're also good with after-dinner coffee.

Makes: **40**

Preparation time: 15 minutes

Cooking time: 10 minutes

40 g/1½ oz Cadbury's Bournville chocolate
40 g/1½ oz caster sugar
½ teaspoon ground cinnamon
350 g/11½ oz puff pastry, thawed if frozen
beaten egg, to glaze
extra caster sugar, for sprinkling

1 Lightly grease a large baking sheet. Grate the chocolate and mix it with the sugar and cinnamon.

2 Roll out the pastry on a lightly floured surface to a 30 cm/12 inch square, then cut it in half. Brush one half with beaten egg and sprinkle the chocolate mixture over the top in an even layer, spreading it to within 5 mm/¼ inch of the edges of the pastry. Brush the other half of the pastry with beaten egg and invert it onto the first half, sandwiching the chocolate mixture. Roll out again to a 30 cm/12 inch square.

3 Cut the pastry in half and brush with beaten egg. Cut each half into strips about 1.5 cm/¾ inch wide. Twist each strip and place on the baking sheet. Brush with beaten egg. Bake in a preheated oven, 220°C (425°F), Gas Mark 7, for 10 minutes or until golden, then dust with caster sugar. Transfer to a wire rack to cool.

Glazed Chocolate Ginger Hearts

These little chocolate-coated spiced biscuits are reminiscent of Lebkuchen, German Christmas biscuits, and would look pretty boxed up as a gift.

Makes: 25

Preparation time: 30 minutes, plus chilling and setting

Cooking time: about 15 minutes

125 g/4 oz unsalted butter, softened
125 g/4 oz caster sugar
1 egg
125 g/4 oz black treacle
400 g/13 oz self-raising flour
2 teaspoons ground ginger
TO DECORATE
200 g/7 oz Cadbury's Bournville chocolate, broken into pieces
200 g/7 oz Cadbury's Dairy Milk chocolate, broken into pieces
½ standard packet Cadbury Land Creamy-White Buttons

1 Beat together the butter and sugar until pale and creamy. Add the egg and treacle. Sift the flour and spice into the bowl and mix all the ingredients together to form a firm dough. Knead lightly and chill for 30 minutes.

2 Lightly grease 2 baking sheets. Roll out the dough to a thickness of 8 mm/⅜ inch and cut out heart shapes, using a biscuit cutter. Transfer the shapes to the baking sheets, spacing them slightly apart. Re-roll the trimmings to make more biscuits. Bake in a preheated oven, 180°C (350°F), Gas Mark 4, for about 10 minutes until slightly risen. Transfer to a wire rack and leave to cool.

3 Melt the plain and milk chocolate in separate bowls. Using a dessertspoon, spoon the plain chocolate over about half the biscuits, reserving a little for decoration. Lay a white chocolate Button in the centre of half the coated biscuits. Use the milk chocolate to cover the remaining biscuits, again reserving a little and laying a white chocolate Button in the centre of half the coated biscuits.

4 Put the reserved milk chocolate in a piping bag fitted with a fine nozzle and pipe wavy lines over the edges of the Buttons on the plain chocolate covered biscuits. Pipe lines back and forth over the remaining biscuits covered with plain chocolate. Use the reserved plain chocolate to decorate the biscuits covered with milk chocolate and Buttons in the same way. Leave to set. Store in a cool dry place for up to 2 days.

Chunky Choc Crumbles

Buttery, crumbly and topped with a thick layer of Cadbury's Dairy Milk chocolate, these little biscuits make a really delicious treat. Leave out the cinnamon if you prefer.

Makes: **12**

Preparation time: 20 minutes

Cooking time: 30 minutes

175 g/6 oz self-raising flour
½ teaspoon ground cinnamon
finely grated rind of 1 lemon
150 g/5 oz firm unsalted butter
60 g/2½ oz caster sugar
1 egg yolk
200 g/7 oz Cadbury's Dairy Milk chocolate, broken into pieces
icing sugar, for dusting (optional)

1 Grease an 18 cm/7 inch square shallow baking tin. Put the flour, cinnamon and rind in a food processor. Add 75 g/3 oz of the butter, cut into small pieces, and blend until the mixture resembles breadcrumbs.

2 Add the sugar and blend until the mixture starts to bind together. Remove 75 g/3 oz of the mixture and reserve. Add the egg yolk to the mixture in the processor and blend to a thick paste. Press the paste into the base of the tin. Bake in a preheated oven, 160°C (325°F), Gas Mark 3, for 15 minutes.

3 Melt the chocolate, then stir in the remaining butter until melted. Spread the chocolate mixture over the mixture in the tin, then scatter the reserved crumble over the top. Bake for 12 minutes more.

4 Leave the biscuit to cool in the tin, then cut into 12 squares. Serve dusted with icing sugar, if liked.

Chocolate Spice Biscuits

These jumbo cookies have a mildly spiced, fruity flavour. Like most biscuits and cookies they won't become crisp until they've cooled, so don't be tempted to overcook them.

Makes: **20**

Preparation time: 15 minutes

Cooking time: 12–15 minutes

150 g/5 oz Cadbury's Bournville chocolate or Cadbury's Dairy Milk chocolate
225 g/7½ oz plain flour
1 teaspoon ground mixed spice
125 g/4 oz firm butter or margarine
125 g/4 oz light muscovado sugar
1 egg
1 egg yolk
100 g/3½ oz mixed dried fruit

1 Lightly grease a large baking sheet. Finely chop the chocolate.

2 Put the flour and spice in a food processor. Add the butter or margarine, cut into small pieces, and blend until the mixture resembles breadcrumbs. Blend in the sugar, egg, egg yolk, dried fruit and chocolate until the mixture starts to bind together.

3 Turn the dough out on to a floured surface and knead lightly. Roll out to a thickness of 5 mm/¼ inch and cut out 20 rounds, using a 7 cm/3 inch biscuit cutter. Place the rounds on the baking sheet.

4 Bake in a preheated oven, 180°C (350°F), Gas Mark 4, for 12–15 minutes until starting to colour around the edges. Leave on the baking sheet for 3 minutes, then transfer to a wire rack to cool.

Mosaic Bars

A scattering of broken creamy-white and milk chocolate Buttons gives these simple biscuits a pretty decoration. Use cinnamon or mixed spice instead of ginger, or leave the spice out altogether if you like.

Makes: **36**

Preparation time: 15 minutes, plus chilling

Cooking time: 8–10 minutes

175 g/6 oz plain flour
1 teaspoon ground ginger
50 g/2 oz firm unsalted butter or margarine
75 g/3 oz dark muscovado sugar
3 tablespoons golden syrup
1 egg yolk
2 standard packets Cadbury Land milk chocolate Buttons
2 standard packets Cadbury Land Creamy-White Buttons

1 Lightly grease a baking sheet. Put the flour and ginger in a food processor. Add the butter or margarine, cut into small pieces, and blend until the mixture resembles breadcrumbs. Add the sugar, golden syrup and egg yolk and blend until the mixture starts to bind together.

2 Turn the dough out on to a lightly floured surface and roll out to a 24 cm/9½ inch square. Chill for at least 30 minutes. Place on the baking sheet.

3 Roughly break up the milk chocolate and creamy-white Buttons into slightly smaller pieces. Scatter the pieces over the biscuit base, then push a rolling pin firmly over the broken Buttons to press them into the base a little.

4 Bake in a preheated oven, 180°C (350°F), Gas Mark 4, for 8–10 minutes, then leave the biscuit on the baking sheet until almost cool. Cut the square in half, then cut each half into 18 bars.

Double Chocolate Sandwiches

For those who like a more traditional chocolate biscuit, these are the perfect choice. They're best eaten within a couple of days of making.

Makes: **15**

Preparation time: 20 minutes

Cooking time: 20 minutes

125 g/4 oz firm unsalted butter or margarine
150 g/5 oz plain flour
2 tablespoons cocoa powder
50 g/2 oz caster sugar
TO FINISH
100 g/3½ oz Cadbury's Dairy Milk chocolate, broken into pieces

1 Grease a large baking sheet. Cut the butter or margarine into small pieces and place in a food processor with the flour and cocoa powder. Blend until the mixture resembles fine breadcrumbs. Stir in the sugar and blend to a firm dough.

2 Turn out on to a lightly floured surface and roll out thinly to a 28 x 20 cm/11 x 8 inch rectangle. Transfer to the prepared baking sheet. Cut lengthways into three long strips, then cut across the strips at 2.5 cm/1 inch intervals to make about 30 small bars. Prick the bars with a fork and bake in a preheated oven, 200°C (400°F), Gas Mark 6, for about 15 minutes until they are just beginning to darken around the edges.

3 While still warm, re-cut the marked lines. Leave on the baking sheet for 2 minutes, then transfer to a wire rack to cool. Melt the chocolate and use to sandwich the biscuits together in pairs. Leave to set.

Chocolate Macaroons

Crisp on the outside and moist inside, little chocolate macaroons make a stylish accompaniment to coffee, either mid-morning or after dinner.

Makes: **about 25**

Preparation time: 10 minutes

Cooking time: 15 minutes

50 g/2 oz Cadbury's Bournville chocolate
2 egg whites
100 g/3½ oz caster sugar
125 g/4 oz ground almonds
about 25 chocolate-flavoured coffee
  beans, to decorate

1 Line a large baking sheet with nonstick baking parchment. Grate the chocolate.
2 Whisk the egg whites until stiff. Gradually whisk in the sugar until the mixture is thick and glossy. Gently fold in the ground almonds and grated chocolate. Put the mixture in a large piping bag fitted with a large plain nozzle and pipe small rounds, about 4 cm/1½ inches in diameter, on to the baking sheet. Alternatively, place small teaspoonfuls on the baking sheet.
3 Press a chocolate-flavoured coffee bean into the centre of each macaroon. Bake in a preheated oven, 180°C (350°F), Gas Mark 4, for about 15 minutes until slightly risen and just firm. Leave the macaroons on the paper to cool. Store in an airtight container.

variation
Chocolate-flavoured coffee beans are available from some supermarkets and coffee specialists. If you can't find a stockist, decorate each biscuit with a whole blanched almond.

no bake cakes

Here is a choice of impressive looking but easy-to-make cakes, in which plain, milk and white chocolate are combined with a variety of other favourite flavours. Whether you prefer smoothness of marshmallows, the unique smoky taste of Irish whiskey, almond-flavoured liqueur or pure orange juice, we have the perfect cake.

Chocolate Biscuit Cake

This is a refrigerator-style cake, so called because the ingredients are chilled, rather than baked, until set. Make sure the chocolate is completely cool before stirring in the other ingredients, then when the cake is sliced, there will be an interesting pattern.

Serves: **12**

Preparation time: 15 minutes, plus cooling and chilling

300 g/10 oz Cadbury's Bournville chocolate, broken into pieces
2 tablespoons milk
125 g/4 oz unsalted butter, melted
125 g/4 oz digestive biscuits
2 standard packets Cadbury Land Creamy-White Buttons
2 standard packets Cadbury Land milk chocolate Buttons

1 Grease and line an 18 cm/7 inch round cake tin. Melt the plain chocolate with the milk, then stir in the butter. Leave until the mixture is cool, but not beginning to solidify.
2 Break the digestive biscuits into small pieces and mix with the creamy-white and milk chocolate Buttons.
3 Stir the biscuit and Button mixture into the chocolate and butter, then turn into the prepared tin and pack it down gently Chill for at least 3 hours until firm.
4 Remove the cake from the tin and peel away the lining paper. Serve sliced into thin wedges.

Irish Coffee Gâteau

A simple dessert for easy entertaining. Make it a day in advance so that it slices neatly.

Serves: **8**

Preparation time: 30 minutes, plus cooling and chilling

2 tablespoons instant coffee granules
100 ml/3½ fl oz hot water
50 g/2 oz caster sugar
3 tablespoons Irish whiskey
300 g/10 oz Cadbury's Bournville chocolate, broken into pieces
300 ml/½ pint double cream
200 g/7 oz Greek yogurt
200 g/7 oz packet Savoiardi biscuits or sponge fingers

TO DECORATE

plain or milk chocolate curls (see page 8)
cocoa powder, for dusting

1 Dissolve the coffee granules in the measured hot water in a saucepan. Add the sugar and heat gently until the sugar dissolves. Bring to the boil and boil rapidly for 1 minute. Remove from the heat and leave to cool. Stir in the whiskey.

2 Put the chocolate in a saucepan with half the cream and heat very gently until the chocolate melts. Remove from the heat and turn into a bowl. Stir in the remaining cream and the yogurt. Leave to thicken slightly.

3 Using a palette knife, spread a thin layer of the chocolate mixture on to the centre of a flat rectangular plate, making a 23 x 10 cm/9 x 4 inch rectangle. Dip one-third of the biscuits in the coffee syrup so they're softened but not too soggy.

4 Arrange the dipped biscuits side by side on the chocolate. Spread a little more chocolate mixture over the biscuits. Dip half the remaining biscuits in the syrup and arrange them as before over the chocolate mixture. Spread more chocolate mixture on top, then cover with the remaining syrup-dipped sponges.

5 Spread the remaining chocolate mixture over the top and sides of the cake to cover it completely, making as smooth as possible with the knife.

6 Chill for 3–4 hours until set. Decorate the top with chocolate curls and serve dusted with cocoa powder.

Chocolate Malt Crunch

As an alternative to setting these little cereal bars in a tin, spoon them into paper cake cases, packing the mixture down lightly.

Makes: **12**

Preparation time: 20 minutes, plus chilling

50 g/2 oz whole almonds
50 g/2 oz shelled peanuts
100 g/3½ oz stoned dates
3 tablespoons malt extract
100 g/3½ oz Cadbury's Bournville chocolate, broken into pieces
25 g/1 oz unsalted butter or margarine
75 g/3 oz bran flakes

1 Lightly grease an 18 cm/7 inch square cake tin. Toast the almonds and peanuts, then coarsely chop them with the dates.

2 Put the malt extract and chocolate in a saucepan and heat very gently until the chocolate melts. Stir in the butter or margarine. Remove from the heat and stir in the nuts, dates and bran flakes until the ingredients are coated in chocolate.
3 Turn the mixture into the prepared tin and pack down to an even layer. Chill for 2 hours until firm. Turn out of the tin and cut into 12 bars.

variation
If you don't like the flavour of malt extract, use golden syrup or treacle instead.

Ricotta, Orange and Chocolate Torte

Ricotta cheese is frequently used in Italian cakes and gâteaux, both baked and unbaked. It's lovely mixed with fruit, spices and chocolate , and perfect if you prefer a dessert that is not too sweet.

Serves: **8–10**

Preparation time: 20 minutes, plus chilling

2 oranges
125 g/4 oz caster sugar
2 pieces (about 25 g/1 oz) stem ginger
75 g/3 oz raisins
200 g/7 oz Cadbury's Bournville chocolate
500 g/1 lb ricotta cheese
150 ml/¼ pint double cream
12 trifle sponges (1½ packets)
cocoa powder, for dusting
pouring cream, to serve

1 Grease and line the sides of a 23 cm/ 9 inch springform cake tin with greaseproof paper. Finely grate the rind of one of the oranges. Squeeze the juice from both oranges and mix with the rind and 50 g/2 oz of the sugar.
2 Finely chop the ginger. Roughly chop the raisins. Grate the chocolate. Beat the ricotta in a bowl, then stir in the ginger, raisins, chocolate and remaining sugar.

3 Lightly whip the cream until slightly thickened, then stir into the mixture.
4 Cut the trifle sponges horizontally into three thin layers. Fit a layer of sponges into the prepared tin, cutting where necessary to fit. Drizzle one-third of the orange syrup over the top. Cover with half of the ricotta mixture, then with half of the remaining sponges. Drizzle more syrup over the sponges, then add the remaining ricotta mixture. Cover with the remaining sponges and syrup. Chill the torte for at least 4 hours or overnight.
5 To serve, remove the sides of the tin and peel away the paper. Invert on to a serving plate and lift away the base. Dust the top generously with cocoa powder. Serve with pouring cream.

Flake and Almond Mallow

This makes a very small, shallow cake, but it is very rich, so keep portions small. It's perfect with after-dinner coffee.

Serves: **8**

Preparation time: 10 minutes, plus chilling

200 g/7 oz Cadbury's Bournville chocolate, broken into pieces
2 tablespoons milk
25 g/1 oz unsalted butter, melted
2 Cadbury's Flake
50 g/2 oz blanched almonds
50 g/2 oz mini marshmallows

1 Dampen a 500 g/1 lb loaf tin, then line with greaseproof paper. Reserve 25 g/1 oz of the plain chocolate. Melt the remainder with the milk, then stir in the butter. Leave until cold but not beginning to solidify.
2 Cut 1 Flake into 1 cm/½ inch lengths. Stir the pieces of Flake, the almonds and marshmallows into the melted chocolate mixture and pack into the prepared tin. Chill for at least 3 hours until set.
3 Remove from the tin and peel away the paper. Melt the reserved chocolate. Cut the remaining Flake lengthways into shards. Using a palette knife, spread the melted chocolate over the top of the cake, then press the Flake shards into it. Chill for a further 15 minutes to set. Remove from the refrigerator 20 minutes before serving. Serve thinly sliced.

variation
For a large gathering, double the quantities used here and use a 1 kg/2 lb loaf tin.

Bournville and Amaretti Slice

Very rich with a hint of alcohol, this blend of crumbly biscuits and velvet smooth chocolate makes a really special cake or dessert to serve with coffee. Make it a day in advance so that it's easy to slice.

Serves: **10**

Preparation time: 20 minutes, plus chilling

175 g/6 oz amaretti biscuits
3 tablespoons almond-flavoured liqueur
275 g/9 oz Cadbury's Bournville chocolate, broken into pieces
300 ml/½ pint double cream
75 g/3 oz unsalted butter, softened
50 g/2 oz caster sugar
TO DECORATE
25 g/1 oz amaretti biscuits, crushed
25 g/1 oz Cadbury's Bournville chocolate

1 Line the base and sides of a lightly greased 500 g/1 lb loaf tin with clingfilm. Crush the biscuits into small pieces. Put the pieces into a bowl and spoon the liqueur over them.
2 Melt the chocolate with half the cream. Cream together the butter and sugar until pale and fluffy. Stir in the chocolate and cream mixture, then the remaining cream.
3 Spoon about one-third of the chocolate mixture into the tin. Scatter half of the biscuit pieces over the top. Spread with half of the remaining chocolate mixture, then add the remaining biscuits. Finish with the remaining chocolate mixture.
4 Chill the chocolate cake overnight until set. Invert on to a plate and peel off the film. To decorate, scatter the top with more crushed biscuits. Melt the chocolate and put it in a piping bag fitted with a fine nozzle. Scribble lines of chocolate over the top of the cake. Serve sliced.

Pyramid Slice

This cake is set in a tilted cake tin to give it an interesting shape. If any pieces of biscuit come above the level of the chocolate mixture, slice them off once the cake has set, so that it sits flat on the plate.

Serves: **10**

Preparation time: 20 minutes, plus cooling and setting

175 g/6 oz digestive biscuits
125 g/4 oz stoned dates, prunes or
  dried apricots
300 g/10 oz Cadbury's Dairy Milk
  chocolate, broken into pieces
100 ml/3½ fl oz evaporated milk
100 g/3½ oz chopped mixed nuts
50 g/2 oz Cadbury's Bournville chocolate,
  broken into pieces

1 Line the base and three sides of a greased deep 18 cm/7 inch square cake tin with clingfilm. Break the biscuits into small pieces. Roughly chop the dried fruit.
2 Put the milk chocolate in a heavy-based saucepan with the evaporated milk and heat very gently, stirring frequently, until the chocolate has melted. Remove from the heat and transfer to a bowl. Leave until cool, but not set.
3 Stir in the pieces of biscuit, the dried fruit and nuts. Prop up one side of the prepared tin on a box so that it sits at an angle of 45 degrees and the unlined side of the tin is uppermost. Spoon in the cake mixture and level the surface. Leave until firm, then transfer to the refrigerator to set completely.
4 Remove the cake from the tin and peel away the film. Melt the plain chocolate. Using a teaspoon, drizzle lines of melted chocolate over the pyramid. Leave to set again, then serve thinly sliced.

iced desserts

Take a day off from calorie counting
and indulge your friends and family
with these mouthwatering chilled
desserts. There are ice creams
both plain and fancy, mousses
and a marquise, and even little
chocolate cups, the ideal container
for the creamiest of orange-
flavoured creams.

Chocolate Prune Marquise

The combination of dark rich chocolate and liqueur-laced prunes is always delicious, particularly in creamy desserts. This special occasion ice cream can be assembled on a serving plate and popped back in the freezer so there's nothing to do at the last minute.

Serves: **8**

Preparation time: 25 minutes, plus cooling and freezing

200 g/7 oz ready-to-eat prunes
200 ml/7 fl oz water
3 tablespoons almond-flavoured liqueur or
  brandy
600 ml/1 pint double cream
2 tablespoons caster sugar
½ teaspoon almond essence
300 g/10 oz Cadbury's Bournville
  chocolate, broken into pieces
50 g/2 oz unsalted butter
TO FINISH
6 amaretti or macaroon biscuits
chocolate shapes (see page 9), to decorate
  (optional)

1 Line the base and sides of a greased 1 kg/2 lb loaf tin with clingfilm. Put the prunes and water in a small, heavy-based saucepan and bring to the boil. Reduce the heat and simmer gently for 3 minutes until the prunes have plumped up slightly. Stir in the liqueur or brandy and leave to cool.

2 Whip half the cream with the sugar and almond essence until the mixture is just holding its shape.

3 Drain the prunes, reserving the liquid. Melt the chocolate with the reserved liquid, then stir in the butter until smooth. Cool slightly.

4 Whip the remaining cream until just peaking. Stir in the chocolate mixture and the prunes until combined. Spoon one-third of the mixture into the base of the prepared tin. Spread half the whipped cream mixture over the top, then half the remaining chocolate mixture. Cover with the remaining cream mixture, and finally with the remaining chocolate mixture. Level the surface and freeze for at least 6 hours or overnight.

5 Crush the amaretti or macaroon biscuits. Invert the ice cream on to a flat freezer-proof serving plate and peel away the clingfilm. Press the crushed biscuits over the ice cream to decorate, then return it to the freezer. Transfer to the refrigerator about 30 minutes before serving. Serve sliced and decorated with chocolate shapes, if you like.

Chocolate Chip Ice Cream

A traditional ice cream, made with an egg custard base, flavoured with Cadbury's Bournville chocolate and little chips of Cadbury's Dairy Milk chocolate. If you have an ice cream maker, use it to give a smooth and creamy result, stirring in the milk chocolate at the end of the churning.

Serves: **4–6**

Preparation time: 30 minutes, plus cooling and freezing

3 egg yolks

50 g/2 oz caster sugar

2 teaspoons cornflour

300 ml/½ pint milk

200 g/7 oz Cadbury's Bournville chocolate, broken into pieces

100 g/3½ oz Cadbury's Dairy Milk chocolate

300 ml/½ pint double cream

chocolate curls, to decorate (see page 8)

1 Beat the egg yolks in a bowl with the sugar, cornflour and a little of the milk. Put the remaining milk in a saucepan and bring to the boil. Pour the hot milk into the egg yolk mixture, stirring. Return the mixture to the saucepan and cook gently, stirring until the custard has thickened enough to thinly coat the back of the spoon. (Do not overheat the mixture or it may curdle.)

2 Remove from the heat and stir in the plain chocolate. Leave until melted, then stir until smooth. Pour into a bowl, cover the surface of the custard with greaseproof paper to prevent a skin forming, and leave to cool.

3 Chop the milk chocolate into fine irregular pieces and reserve. Whisk the cream into the cold custard. Turn the mixture into a freezer container and freeze for 2–3 hours or until the ice cream has frozen around the edges.

4 Spoon the ice cream into a bowl and mash with a fork to break down the ice crystals. Return to the freezer for a further 2 hours or until it has frozen around the edges again. Repeat the process once or twice more, stirring in the milk chocolate pieces at this stage. Return to the freezer.

5 Transfer the ice cream to the refrigerator about 45 minutes before serving. Serve scooped into glasses and decorate with chocolate curls.

Rocky Road Ice Cream

For this simple American-style dessert use good quality bought ice cream. It will save time, and the flavour will be enhanced by folding in all the extra goodies. Serve with chocolate sauce (see page 23) or scatter chocolate shavings (see page 8) over each serving.

Serves: **6**

Preparation time: 10 minutes, plus softening and freezing

1 litre/1¾ pints good quality vanilla ice cream
2 Cadbury's Crunchie bars
3 standard packets Cadbury Land Creamy-White Buttons
75 g/3 oz mini marshmallows
50 g/2 oz raisins

1 Transfer the ice cream to the refrigerator for 30–60 minutes to let it soften slightly.

2 Meanwhile, chop the Crunchie bars into small irregular pieces, reserving all the crumbs. Lightly crush the Buttons while still in their packets to break them into slightly smaller pieces. Mix together the Crunchie and chocolate Button pieces, the marshmallows and raisins.

3 Turn the ice cream into a bowl and break it up with a spoon. Add the other ingredients to the bowl and mix together until well dispersed in the ice cream. Transfer to an ice cream container and return to the freezer for several hours or overnight. Serve spooned into glasses.

Neapolitan Whirl

This is a really easy ice cream made with whipped cream. You can easily substitute strawberries for the raspberries. Purée 225 g/7½ oz fresh strawberries, then press them through a sieve.

Serves: **8**

Preparation time: 20 minutes, plus cooling and freezing

225 g/7½ oz raspberries
175 g/6 oz caster sugar
150 ml/¼ pint water
200 g/7 oz Cadbury's Bournville chocolate, broken into pieces
600 ml/1 pint double cream

1 Press the raspberries through a sieve to make a purée. Heat the sugar and water in a saucepan until the sugar dissolves. Bring to the boil and boil for 2 minutes until syrupy. Leave to cool.
2 Melt the chocolate with 150 ml/¼ pint of the cream. Stir until smooth, then cool slightly. Whip the remaining cream with the cooled syrup until softly peaking. Spoon half the cream and syrup mixture into a separate bowl and fold in the raspberry purée. Half fold the chocolate mixture into the remaining cream and syrup mixture until marbled.
3 Place alternate spoonfuls of the raspberry and chocolate mixtures in a freezer container. Using a large metal spoon, fold the mixtures together two or three times until slightly mingled. Freeze overnight until firm.
4 Transfer the ice cream to the refrigerator about 30 minutes before serving. Serve scooped into bowls.

Iced Chocolate Mousse

Lightened with whipped cream and egg whites, this rich iced dessert has a mousse-like texture. Here it's frozen in little pudding moulds, then turned out for serving, but you can freeze it in ramekin dishes or even in a tub to serve it in scoops like ice cream.

Serves: **6**

Preparation time: 20 minutes, plus cooling and freezing

300 g/10 oz Cadbury's Bournville chocolate, broken into pieces
3 tablespoons golden syrup
2 tablespoons brandy, orange-flavoured liqueur or water
5 tablespoons water
100 g/3½ oz cocoa powder
300 ml/½ pint whipping cream
4 egg whites
2 tablespoons caster sugar
pouring cream, to serve

1 Melt the chocolate with the golden syrup, brandy, liqueur or water, plus the 5 tablespoons water. Stir until smooth, then stir in the cocoa powder. Pour into a large bowl and leave until cold.

2 Whip the cream until just peaking. Whisk the egg whites in a separate bowl until stiff, then gradually whisk in the sugar.

3 Using a large metal spoon, fold the whipped cream and then the egg whites into the chocolate mixture until evenly combined. Spoon into 6 individual metal pudding moulds or dariole moulds and freeze for at least 4 hours.

4 To serve, dip the moulds very briefly in hot water. Run a small knife around the edge of each mousse to check that it has loosened from the mould. Tap out on to serving plates. Serve with pouring cream.

Black Forest Ice Cream

Serves: **6–8**

Preparation time: 20 minutes, plus cooling and freezing

425 g/14 oz can pitted black cherries in syrup
1 tablespoon cornflour
125 g/4 oz luxury double chocolate cookies
2 Cadbury's Flake
200 g/7 oz Cadbury's Bournville chocolate, broken into pieces
450 ml/¾ pint double cream
2 tablespoons icing sugar
2 teaspoons vanilla essence
200 g/7 oz Greek yogurt
fresh cherries, to decorate (optional)

1 Drain the cherries, reserving the syrup. Blend a little of the syrup in a small saucepan with the cornflour. Stir in the remaining syrup and bring to the boil, stirring until thickened. Cook gently for 1 minute. Remove from the heat, stir in the cherries and leave to cool.

2 Put the chocolate cookies in a polythene bag and tap them gently with a rolling pin to break into small pieces. Crumble the Flake into chunky pieces.

3 Melt the chocolate with 75 ml/3 fl oz of the cream. Stir until smooth and leave to cool slightly. Whip the remaining cream in a bowl with the icing sugar, vanilla essence and yogurt until the cream just starts to hold its shape. Stir in half the chocolate mixture. Gently fold in the pieces of cookie and Flake.

4 Place spoonfuls of the remaining chocolate mixture and the cherries in syrup over the cream mixture. Using a large metal spoon, fold all the ingredients together until combined but still slightly rippled. Turn into a freezer container and freeze for at least 4 hours.

5 Transfer the ice cream to the refrigerator about 30 minutes before serving. Spoon into glasses and decorate with a few cherries, if liked.

Chocolate and Mascarpone Ice

Creamy mascarpone blended with sugar syrup, plain chocolate and chocolate coffee beans makes a really easy iced dessert. Be sure to use solid dark chocolate coffee beans rather than chocolate-coated coffee beans, which would be far too crunchy. Serve in small portions, because it's very rich.

Serves: **6**

Preparation time: 30 minutes, plus cooling and freezing

250 g/8 oz caster sugar
375 ml/13 fl oz water
300 g/10 oz Cadbury's Bournville chocolate, chopped
75 g/3 oz chocolate coffee beans
250 g/8 oz mascarpone cheese
2 tablespoons lemon juice
300 ml/½ pint whipping cream
4 tablespoons coffee liqueur

1 Put 25 g/1 oz of the sugar in a heavy-based saucepan with 150 ml/¼ pint of the water. Heat gently until the sugar dissolves, then bring to the boil and boil rapidly for 3 minutes. Transfer to a bowl, stir in the chopped chocolate and leave until melted. (If the syrup cools before the chocolate has melted, pop it briefly in the microwave.)

2 Reserve 25 g/1 oz of the chocolate coffee beans. Finely chop the remainder. Beat the mascarpone in a bowl until softened. Stir in the lemon juice and melted chocolate mixture. Whip the cream until just peaking and fold into the mascarpone and chocolate mixture. Fold in the chopped chocolate coffee beans. Turn into a freezer container and freeze for at least 4 hours until firm.

3 For the coffee syrup, heat the remaining sugar and the remaining water in a small heavy-based saucepan until the sugar dissolves. Bring to the boil and boil for 5 minutes until syrupy. Remove from the heat and stir in the coffee liqueur. Leave to cool, then chill until ready to serve.

4 Transfer the ice cream to the refrigerator about 30 minutes before serving. Stir the reserved coffee beans into the syrup. Scoop the ice cream on to serving plates, spoon the coffee syrup over the ice cream and serve immediately.

Flake and Orange Cups

Orange and chocolate-flavoured creams look really stunning nestled inside pretty collars of melted chocolate. They are a special dinner-party dessert and can be frozen well ahead.

Serves: **6**

Preparation time: 40 minutes, plus chilling and freezing

CUPS

225 g/7½ oz Cadbury's Bournville chocolate, broken into pieces

FILLING

200 g/7 oz full fat cream cheese

150 ml/¼ pint double cream

150 g/5 oz natural yogurt

3 tablespoons caster sugar

finely grated rind and juice of 1 orange

3 tablespoons orange-flavoured liqueur (optional)

4 Cadbury's Flake

strips of candied orange peel, to decorate

1 To make the cups, first cut out 6 strips of nonstick baking parchment, each 30 x 5 cm/12 x 2 inches. Line a baking sheet with nonstick baking parchment. Roll up one strip of baking parchment and place inside a 6 cm/2½ inch pastry cutter set on the baking sheet. Open out the strip so it lines the cutter.

2 Melt the chocolate. Spoon a little melted chocolate into the cutter then, holding the cutter in place with one hand, brush the chocolate up the side of the paper to make a chocolate cup with an irregular edge around the top. Carefully lift away the pastry cutter and make 5 more cups in the same way. Chill until set.

3 For the filling, beat the cream cheese in a bowl to soften. Beat in the cream, yogurt, sugar, orange rind and juice and liqueur if using. Cut 1 Flake lengthways into shards and reserve the best pieces for decoration. Crumble the trimmings and the remaining 3 Flake into the creamed mixture.

4 Spoon the mixture into the chocolate cups and freeze for at least 3 hours. Carefully peel away the paper cases and transfer the cups to the refrigerator for about 1 hour before serving. Alternatively, return the cups to the freezer for a later date. Serve the cups decorated with shards of Flake and strips of candied orange peel.

variation
The chocolate cups look really stunning, but if you haven't got time to make them, use bought chocolate cases, available from supermarkets.

hot puddings

Here, chocolate adds a new twist to favourite old-fashioned puddings with a chocolate bread and butter pudding, a sticky upside-down pudding and a chocolate and cardamom rice pudding. Amongst the other goodies are some delicious combinations of chocolate and fruit, a velvety chocolate sauce and the wickedest of wicked chocolate puddings.

Chocolate Pear Slice

This quick and easy dessert is smart enough to serve for a special occasion, and not too heavy if rich courses have preceded it. It can be prepared in advance and cooked just before serving.

Serves: **6**

Preparation time: 30 minutes

Cooking time: about 30 minutes

150 g/5 oz Cadbury's Bournville chocolate, broken into pieces
2 large ripe pears
2 tablespoons lemon juice
340 g/11½ oz puff pastry, thawed if frozen
beaten egg, to glaze
icing sugar, for dusting
pouring cream, to serve

1 Grease a baking sheet and sprinkle with water. Melt the chocolate.
2 Quarter, core and thinly slice the pears. Put the pear slices in a bowl of water along with the lemon juice. Roll out the pastry on a lightly floured surface to a 30 x 18 cm/12 x 7 inch rectangle, trimming the edges neatly. Using the tip of a sharp knife, make a shallow cut along each side, 1 cm/½ inch from the pastry edges.
3 Spread the melted chocolate to within 1 cm/½ inch of the cut line. Thoroughly drain the pears and arrange the slices in overlapping lines over the chocolate, keeping them just inside the cut line. Mark small indentations on the edges of the pastry with the back edge of the knife. Brush the pastry edges with beaten egg, then bake in a preheated oven, 200°C (400°F), Gas Mark 6, for about 25 minutes until the pastry is risen and golden. Remove from the oven.
4 Raise the oven temperature to 230°C (450°F), Gas Mark 8. Generously dust the pastry and pears with icing sugar and return to the oven for about 5 minutes until deep golden, watching closely. Leave to cool slightly, then serve warm with pouring cream.

Warm Scones with Chocolate, Bananas and Maple Syrup

It's worth keeping some bought or homemade drop scones in the freezer for this really quick and easy dessert.

Serves: **4**

Preparation time: 10 minutes

Cooking time: 2–3 minutes

2 large bananas
2 teaspoons lemon juice
100 g/3½ oz Cadbury's Dairy Milk chocolate, finely chopped
4 large drop scones or Scotch pancakes
4 tablespoons maple syrup
lightly whipped cream, or Greek yogurt, to serve

1 Thinly slice the bananas and toss them with the lemon juice. Stir the chocolate into the bananas.

2 Place the drop scones or Scotch pancakes under a grill preheated to moderate for 1–2 minutes until beginning to crisp. Turn them over and pile the chocolate and banana mixture on to the centre of each. Return to the grill for 1 minute further until warmed through.

3 Transfer to serving plates and pour the maple syrup over the top. Serve with lightly whipped cream or Greek yogurt.

Baked Crêpes with Glossy Chocolate Sauce

This recipe uses bought crêpes filled with a creamy ricotta, white chocolate and blueberry mixture and served with lashings of chocolate sauce. Homemade crêpes, can be used instead, of course.

Serves: **4**

Preparation time: 20 minutes

Cooking time: about 12 minutes

250 g/8 oz ricotta cheese
3 tablespoons caster sugar
150 g/5 oz fresh or frozen blueberries, thawed
3 standard packets of Cadbury Land Creamy-White Buttons
4 tablespoons double cream
4 large or 8 small crêpes
SAUCE
125 g/4 oz caster sugar
100 ml/3½ fl oz water
200 g/7 oz Cadbury's Bournville chocolate, broken into pieces
25 g/1 oz unsalted butter

1 Lightly grease a large, shallow ovenproof dish. For the filling, mix together the ricotta, sugar, blueberries, Buttons and cream.

2 Thinly spread the filling over the crêpes, then fold them into quarters and arrange in the prepared dish. Cook in a preheated oven, 190°C (375°F), Gas Mark 5, for 8–10 minutes until warmed through.

3 Meanwhile, for the sauce, heat the caster sugar and water in a small heavy-based saucepan until the sugar is dissolved. Bring to the boil and boil rapidly for 1 minute. Remove from the heat and add the chocolate. Leave until melted, then stir in the butter to make a smooth, glossy sauce. Serve hot, with the crêpes.

Chocolate and Almond Filo Slice

Pieces of Cadbury's Bournville chocolate and a smooth almond paste encased between layers of filo pastry make an easy dessert, whatever the occasion. Serve sliced in small portions because it's very rich, with lightly whipped cream or vanilla ice cream.

Serves: **8–10**

Preparation time: 20 minutes

Cooking time: 25 minutes

200 g/7 oz Cadbury's Bournville chocolate
200 g/7 oz white almond paste
50 g/2 oz unsalted butter
150 g/5 oz filo pastry (about 9 sheets),
  thawed if frozen
cocoa powder, for dusting

1 Chop the chocolate into small pieces. Coarsely grate the almond paste. Melt the butter and brush a little of it over a 35 x 10 cm/14 x 4 inch loose-based rectangular tin.

2 Use one-third of the pastry sheets to line the base and sides of the tin, overlapping them to fit in an even layer and letting the excess pastry overhang the edges. Brush each sheet with butter as you work. Scatter half the grated chocolate and half the almond paste over the pastry.

3 Cover with 3 more sheets of pastry, brushing each lightly with butter. Add the remaining chocolate and almond paste. Cover with 2 more sheets of pastry, then fold all the overhanging pastry into the centre of the tart. Crumple up the final sheet of pastry and lay it over the surface to make a decorative finish.

4 Brush with any remaining butter and bake in a preheated oven, 190°C (375°F), Gas Mark 5, for about 25 minutes until the pastry is deep golden. Leave to cool for 10 minutes, then dust with cocoa powder and serve sliced.

variation
If you don't have a long narrow tin, use a 20 cm/8 inch round loose-based flan tin and serve the dessert sliced into wedges.

Wicked Chocolate Pudding

This is an indulgent steamed pudding for cold winter days. It's rich and chocolatey, and topped with a buttery date and orange sauce.

Serves: **6**

Preparation time: 20 minutes

Cooking time: about 2 hours

75 g/3 oz unsalted butter or margarine, softened
150 g/5 oz light muscovado sugar
finely grated rind of 1 orange
2 eggs
150 g/5 oz self-raising flour
25 g/1 oz cocoa powder
½ teaspoon bicarbonate of soda
100 g/3½ oz Cadbury's Dairy Milk chocolate, chopped
pouring cream or custard, to serve
SAUCE
125 g/4 oz light muscovado sugar
75 g/3 oz unsalted butter
4 tablespoons orange juice
50 g/2 oz stoned dates, chopped

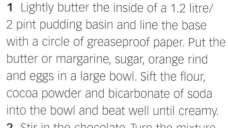

1 Lightly butter the inside of a 1.2 litre/ 2 pint pudding basin and line the base with a circle of greaseproof paper. Put the butter or margarine, sugar, orange rind and eggs in a large bowl. Sift the flour, cocoa powder and bicarbonate of soda into the bowl and beat well until creamy.
2 Stir in the chocolate. Turn the mixture into the prepared basin and level the surface. Cover with a double thickness of greaseproof paper and a sheet of foil, securing them under the rim of the basin with string.
3 Bring a 5 cm/2 inch depth of water to the boil in a large saucepan. Lower in the pudding and cover with a lid. Steam for 1¾ hours, topping up the water occasionally, if necessary.
4 Meanwhile, make the sauce. Put the sugar, butter and orange juice in a small saucepan and heat gently until the sugar dissolves. Bring to the boil and boil for 1 minute. Stir in the chopped dates and cook for 1 minute. To serve, invert the pudding on to a serving plate and pour the sauce over the top. Serve with pouring cream or custard.

Chocolate Sauce Pudding

This classic favourite cannot be beaten for its delicious 'chocolate sauce' flavour. Simply serve warm with plenty of lightly whipped cream.

Serves: **4–6**

Preparation time: 20 minutes

Cooking time: 35 minutes

250 g/8 oz Cadbury's Bournville chocolate, broken into pieces
300 ml/½ pint milk
50 g/2 oz unsalted butter or margarine, softened
150 g/5 oz light muscovado sugar
2 eggs, separated
25 g/1 oz self-raising flour
25 g/1 oz cocoa powder
cocoa powder, for dusting

1 Put the chocolate and milk in a saucepan and heat gently until the chocolate has melted. Remove from the heat and stir until smooth.

2 Beat together the butter or margarine and sugar until pale and creamy. Beat in the egg yolks, flour, cocoa powder and melted chocolate mixture until smooth.
3 In a separate bowl, whisk the egg whites until stiff. Using a large metal spoon, fold the egg whites into the chocolate mixture. Turn into a 1.5 litre/2½ pint pie dish and stand the dish in a roasting tin. Pour a 2.5 cm/1 inch depth of boiling water into the tin.
4 Bake in a preheated oven, 180°C (350°F), Gas Mark 4, for 30 minutes or until the pudding has a crust but is still slightly soft underneath. Serve dusted with cocoa powder.

Warm Chocolate Slice

Although easy to make, this moist, shallow cake is good enough to serve for a special occasion. It really is best warm, so if you make it ahead, pop it back in a moderate oven for about 10 minutes before serving. Chilled crème fraîche is the ideal accompaniment.

Serves: **6**

Preparation time: 20 minutes

Cooking time: about 40–45 minutes

100 g/3½ oz Cadbury's Bournville chocolate, broken into pieces
75 g/3 oz unsalted butter, melted
3 large eggs, separated
125 g/4 oz caster sugar
25 g/1 oz plain flour
75 g/3 oz walnuts, chopped
icing sugar, for dusting
cocoa powder, for dusting

1 Grease and line the base of a 20 cm/8 inch springform or loose-based cake tin. Melt the chocolate, then stir in the butter.
2 Whisk the egg yolks and sugar until pale in colour. Gradually beat in the chocolate mixture, then stir in the flour.

3 In a separate bowl, whisk the egg whites until stiff. Using a large metal spoon, fold into the chocolate mixture. Turn into the prepared tin and sprinkle the walnuts over the top. Bake in a preheated oven, 180°C (350°F), Gas Mark 4, for 35–40 minutes until risen and only just firm in the centre. Leave to cool slightly, then serve warm, dusted with icing sugar and cocoa powder.

Chocolate Bread and Butter Pudding

Anyone who likes bread and butter pudding will adore this irresistible version, which has pockets of chocolate sauce hidden between the layers of bread. For a change, it can be made using slices of brioche or even thinly sliced fruit buns.

Serves: **6**

Preparation time: 20 minutes, plus standing

Cooking time: 50 minutes

250 g/8 oz Cadbury's Bournville chocolate, broken into pieces
60 g/2½ oz unsalted butter
250 g/8 oz spiced fruit bread
3 eggs
25 g/1 oz caster sugar
600 ml/1 pint milk
icing sugar, for dusting

1 Lightly grease a 1.8 litre/3 pint shallow ovenproof dish. Melt the chocolate, then stir in 40 g/1½ oz of the butter to make a thick sauce.

2 Thinly slice the bread and arrange one-third of the slices in the prepared dish. Place spoonfuls of the chocolate sauce over the bread, keeping half the sauce to add to the second layer of bread slices.

3 Cover with half of the remaining bread slices, then add spoonfuls of the remaining chocolate sauce. Arrange the remaining bread slices on top.

4 Melt the remaining butter and beat with the eggs, sugar and milk. Pour the mixture over the pudding and leave for 30 minutes so that the bread swells and absorbs some of the liquid.

5 Bake in a preheated oven, 180°C (350°F), Gas Mark 4, for about 45 minutes until the surface is turning crisp and golden. Serve the pudding warm, dusted with icing sugar.

Grilled Peaches with Chocolate Nut Paste

This not-too-rich pudding is best in summer, when peaches are juicy and ripe. It also works really well with nectarines or very ripe, soft pears.

Serves: **4**

Preparation time: 5 minutes

Cooking time: 5 minutes

4 ripe peaches
100 g/3½ oz Cadbury's Bournville chocolate
50 g/2 oz white almond paste
finely grated rind of 1 lemon
2 tablespoons flaked almonds
4 tablespoons double cream
2 tablespoons icing sugar
pouring cream, to serve

1 Halve the peaches and remove the stones. Arrange the peaches, cut sides up, in a shallow flameproof dish. If the peach halves don't sit upright, take a small slice off the rounded sides.

2 Chop the chocolate and almond paste and divide the mixture among the peach halves. Scatter the lemon rind and almonds over the top and pour over the cream. Dust with icing sugar.

3 Grill under a preheated medium grill for about 5 minutes until the peaches are lightly coloured. Serve warm, with plenty of pouring cream.

Chocolate, Cinnamon and Apple Strudel

The combination of warm chocolate, apples, mild spice and nuts is absolutely delicious, particularly if you serve the strudel with vanilla ice cream or lightly whipped double cream. Filo pastry sheets vary in size depending on the brand used. If the sheets are very narrow, you might need to use extra sheets, overlapping them slightly.

Serves: **6–8**

Preparation time: 25 minutes

Cooking time: 35 minutes

1 kg/2 lb cooking apples
1 tablespoon lemon juice
125 g/4 oz unsalted butter
50 g/2 oz coarse breadcrumbs
½ teaspoon ground cinnamon
50 g/2 oz caster sugar
50 g/2 oz sultanas or raisins
50 g/2 oz chopped hazelnuts
150 g/5 oz Cadbury's Bournville chocolate, chopped
6 sheets filo pastry
icing sugar, for dusting

1 Lightly grease a large baking sheet. Peel, core and slice the apples and put the slices in a bowl of water with the lemon juice to prevent discoloration.

2 Melt 50 g/2 oz of the butter in a frying pan and fry the breadcrumbs for 2–3 minutes until pale golden. Transfer to a large bowl. Thoroughly drain the apples and add them to the bowl with the cinnamon, sugar, sultanas or raisins, hazelnuts and chocolate.

3 Melt the remaining butter. Lay 1 sheet of the pastry on the work surface and brush with a little melted butter. Put another sheet of pastry on top and brush with more butter. Cover with a third sheet of pastry and spoon half the filling down the centre of the pastry to within 2.5 cm/1 inch of the edges.

4 Fold the short ends of the pastry over the filling, then roll up the filling in the pastry like a Swiss roll. Transfer the strudel to the baking sheet with the join underneath. Use the remaining pastry and filling to make another strudel in the same way. Brush both strudels with the remaining butter and bake in a preheated oven, 190°C (375°F), Gas Mark 5, for about 30 minutes until golden. Dust with icing sugar and serve sliced.

Sticky Upside-down Pudding

An old-fashioned pudding that always looks impressive when turned out to reveal pretty pieces of pineapple, bathed in golden syrup.

Serves: **6**

Preparation time: 30 minutes

Cooking time: 35–40 minutes

7 tablespoons golden syrup
425 g/14 oz can pineapple rings
200 g/7 oz Cadbury's Bournville chocolate, broken into pieces
125 g/4 oz unsalted butter or margarine, melted
2 eggs
40 g/1½ oz caster sugar
25 g/1 oz stem ginger from a jar (about 2 pieces), chopped
125 g/4 oz self-raising flour
25 g/1 oz cocoa powder
vanilla ice cream or custard, to serve

1 Grease a 1.4 litre/2½ pint shallow ovenproof dish and line the base with greaseproof paper. Spoon the golden syrup over the base of the dish. Thoroughly drain the pineapple rings and arrange them over the syrup. Melt the chocolate, then stir in the butter or margarine and leave to cool slightly.

2 Put the eggs, sugar, stem ginger and melted chocolate mixture in a bowl. Sift the flour and cocoa powder into the bowl. Beat well until smooth and creamy. Spoon the mixture over the pineapple and level the surface.

3 Bake in a preheated oven, 190°C (375°F), Gas Mark 5, for 35–40 minutes until just firm in the centre. Leave for 5 minutes, then invert on to a serving plate. Remove the greaseproof paper. Serve with ice cream or custard.

variations
This recipe works equally well with canned apricots or pears, arranged cut-side down. You can also add a handful of chopped nuts or sultanas to the sponge mixture, or use maple syrup instead of the golden syrup.

Chocolate Mallow Cups

You can assemble and freeze these puddings in advance, then transfer them to the refrigerator 30 minutes before cooking.

Serves: **6**

Preparation time: 20 minutes

Cooking time: about 8–10 minutes

100 g/3½ oz Cadbury's Bournville chocolate, broken into pieces
40 g/1½ oz unsalted butter
approx 500 ml/17 fl oz good quality vanilla ice cream
25 g/1 oz flaked almonds, lightly toasted
2 egg whites
100 g/3½ oz caster sugar

1 Melt the chocolate, then stir in the butter and leave to cool. Pack the ice cream into 6 ovenproof cups or dishes and scatter two-thirds of the almonds over the top.

2 Spoon the melted chocolate over the ice cream and put the filled cups or dishes in the freezer while making the meringue. Whisk the egg whites until stiff. Gradually whisk in the caster sugar, 1 tablespoonful at a time, until stiff and glossy. Spoon the meringue over the chocolate sauce, piling it up in the centre. Scatter the remaining almonds over the top. Return to the freezer.

3 To serve, bake the cups in a preheated oven, 220°C (425°F), Gas Mark 7, for about 4 minutes until the meringue is turning golden, watching closely towards the end of the cooking time. Serve immediately.

Chocolate and Cardamom Rice Pudding

Cardamom adds an exotic flavour to even the simplest of dishes, so this is a perfect choice if you're looking for more adventurous chocolate combinations. It can be made equally successfully without the cardamom.

Serves: **4**

Preparation time: 15 minutes

Cooking time: about 1½ hours

1 tablespoon green cardamom pods
600 ml/1 pint milk
100 g/3½ oz Cadbury's Bournville
  chocolate, broken into pieces
50 g/2 oz pudding rice
40 g/1½ oz caster sugar

1 Lightly butter a 1.2 litre/2 pint ovenproof dish. Pound the cardamom pods using a pestle and mortar to release their seeds. Discard the pods and crush the seeds until broken down a little.
2 Bring the milk almost to the boil in a saucepan. Remove from the heat, add the chocolate, rice, sugar and cardamom seeds and stir well. Leave for a couple of minutes to allow the chocolate to melt, then stir until combined.
3 Pour into the prepared dish and bake in a preheated oven, 150°C (300°F), Gas Mark 2, for 1½ hours or until the rice is tender. Serve warm.

Chocolate, Maple and Pecan Tart

This superb tart is similar to a classic pecan pie, but with the added bonus of a Bournville chocolate filling. It's good served warm with vanilla ice cream or custard, or chilled and accompanied by crème fraîche or pouring cream.

Serves: **8**

Preparation time: 30 minutes

Cooking time: about 35–40 minutes

200 g/7 oz Cadbury's Bournville chocolate, broken into pieces
50 g/2 oz unsalted butter
75 g/3 oz caster sugar
175 ml/6 fl oz maple syrup
3 eggs
350 g/11½ oz puff pastry or dessert shortcrust pastry, thawed if frozen
125 g/4 oz pecan nuts
icing sugar, for dusting

1 Preheat the oven to 180°C (350°F), Gas Mark 4, and put a baking sheet in the oven, to heat through. Melt the chocolate, then stir in the butter. Put the sugar and maple syrup in a saucepan and heat gently until the sugar dissolves. Leave to cool slightly.

2 Lightly whisk the eggs to a smooth consistency. Whisk in the chocolate and syrup mixtures.

3 Roll out the pastry on a lightly floured surface and use to line a loose-based flan tin, measuring 23 cm/9 inches across the base and 3 cm/1¼ inches deep. Pour the filling into the pastry case. Place on the hot baking sheet and bake for 15 minutes until the filling is just beginning to set.

4 Remove the tart from the oven and scatter the pecan nuts over the top. Bake for a further 10 minutes until the nuts are beginning to brown. Remove from the oven and raise the temperature to 230°C (450°F), Gas Mark 8. Dust the tart generously with icing sugar and return to the oven for about 5 minutes until the nuts are beginning to caramelize. Leave to cool for 20 minutes before serving.

Chocolate and Almond Sponge Pudding

A dream of a pudding for chocolate fans, this rich chocolate steamed pudding hides a buttery chocolate and almond paste centre.

Serves: **6**

Preparation time: 20 minutes

Cooking time: 2 hours

75 g/3 oz unsalted butter
60 g/2½ oz ground almonds
½ teaspoon almond essence
25 g/1 oz caster sugar
100 g/3½ oz Cadbury's Bournville chocolate

SPONGE
100 g/3½ oz Cadbury's Bournville chocolate, broken into pieces
75 g/3 oz unsalted butter
225 g/7½ oz self-raising flour
25 g/1 oz cocoa powder
150 g/5 oz caster sugar
2 eggs
2 tablespoons milk
pouring cream or custard, to serve

1 Butter the inside of a 1.2 litre/2 pint pudding basin. For the filling, melt the butter in a small saucepan, then stir in the almonds, almond essence and sugar. Chop the chocolate and stir it in to make a paste.

2 For the sponge, melt the chocolate, then stir in the butter to make a sauce and cool slightly. Sift the flour and cocoa powder into a bowl. Add the sugar, eggs, milk and chocolate mixture and stir the ingredients together until just combined.

3 Spoon about two-thirds of the mixture into the basin, making a deep well in the centre, then spoon in the filling. Cover with the remaining sponge mixture. Cover with a double thickness of greaseproof paper and a sheet of foil, securing them under the rim of the basin with string.

4 Bring a 5 cm/2 inch depth of water to the boil in a large saucepan. Lower in the pudding and cover with a lid. Steam for 1¾ hours, topping up the water occasionally, if necessary.

5 Turn off the heat and leave to cool for 15 minutes. Invert the pudding on to a plate. Serve with cream or custard.

Flake Baked Bananas

This is the easiest dessert imaginable. Bananas are split lengthways and each one stuffed with a Cadbury's Flake. Serve with chocolate sauce, cream or ice cream.

Serves: **4**

Preparation time: 5 minutes

Cooking time: 20–25 minutes

4 bananas
4 Cadbury's Flake

1 Leaving the skins on, cut a deep slit down the length of each banana. Open out the bananas and press a Flake into each. Wrap individually in foil.

2 Bake in a preheated oven, 180°C (350°F), Gas Mark 4, for 20–25 minutes until the bananas are tender. Serve warm.

Baked Pears with Chocolate Sauce

For this simple dessert you need juicy, plump pears. Under-ripe pears will take too long to bake and the melted chocolate 'stuffing' will spoil.

Serves: **4**

Preparation time: 20 minutes

Cooking time: 20 minutes

75 g/3 oz Cadbury's Bournville chocolate
15 g/½ oz firm unsalted butter
25 g/1 oz sultanas
25 g/1 oz chopped roasted hazelnuts or mixed nuts
4 pears
2 tablespoons golden syrup
pouring cream, to serve

1 Lightly butter a small ovenproof dish. Finely chop the chocolate and the butter. Mix together with the sultanas and nuts.
2 Cut a thin slice off the base of the pears to make them stand upright. Slice 1.5 cm/¾ inch off the top of each pear and retain for use as lids. Using a small sharp knife, cut out the core almost down to the base of each pear, working from the top so that the pears remain intact. (Alternatively, core the pears with an apple corer, then 'plug' the bases with the core ends and scoop out a little more of each pear with a knife or teaspoon.)
3 Pack the chocolate mixture into the pears and place them in the dish with the lids. Add 4 tablespoons water and cover with foil. Bake in a preheated oven, 180°C (350°F), Gas Mark 4, for 10 minutes until the chocolate mixture sinks down into the pears.
4 Pack any remaining chocolate mixture into the pears and pour the golden syrup over the top. Bake for a further 10 minutes until the pears are tender. Position the lids and serve warm, with pouring cream.

Chocolate Custard

For texture and flavour, real homemade custard is simply unbeatable. Serve with warm or cold poached fruits, or poured over steamed chocolate puddings or pastries.

Serves: **4**

Preparation time: 10 minutes

Cooking time: 6–8 minutes

3 egg yolks
1 tablespoon caster sugar
2 teaspoons cornflour
300 ml/½ pint milk
75 g/3 oz Cadbury's Bournville chocolate, chopped
4 tablespoons double cream

1 Whisk the egg yolks in a bowl with the sugar, cornflour and a little of the milk.
2 Put the remaining milk in a heavy-based saucepan and bring just to the boil. Pour the milk over the egg-yolk mixture, whisking well, then pour the custard back into the pan.
3 Cook over a gentle heat, stirring until the custard thinly coats the back of a wooden spoon. (Do not allow it to boil or it may curdle.)
4 Remove from the heat and add the chocolate. Leave until melted, then add the cream and stir until smooth. Pour into a serving jug.

variations
For a mocha-flavoured custard, whisk 1 tablespoon coffee granules or 2 tablespoons espresso coffee powder with the egg yolks.

special occasion desserts and gâteaux

These desserts and gâteaux are designed to make the sort of spectacular finales to a meal that will guarantee you curtain calls. Chocolate is combined with truffles, with strawberrries, cream and meringue, with passionfruit and with other delectable favourites to add up to some of the most indulgent but thoroughly enjoyable chocolate treats imaginable.

Chocolate Filigree Torte

An impressive gâteau of silky smooth chocolate and mascarpone creams set between thin layers of light chocolate sponge.

Serves: **10**

Preparation time: 30 minutes, plus cooling and chilling

Cooking time: 20–25 minutes

3 eggs
75 g/3 oz caster sugar
50 g/2 oz plain flour
25 g/1 oz cocoa powder
FILLING
2 teaspoons powdered gelatine
3 tablespoons cold water
200 g/7 oz Cadbury's Bournville chocolate, broken into pieces
500 g/1 lb mascarpone cheese, at room temperature
75 g/3 oz caster sugar
1 teaspoon vanilla essence
200 g/7 oz Greek yogurt
4 tablespoons hot water

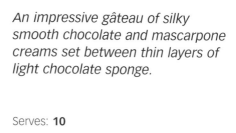

1 Grease and line a 23 cm/9 inch springform or loose-based cake tin. Put the eggs and sugar in a heatproof bowl over a pan of hot water. Whisk until the mixture is thickened and the beaters leave a trail when lifted from the bowl.

2 Remove from the heat and whisk for a further 2 minutes. Sift the flour and cocoa powder over the mixture, then fold in using a large metal spoon. Turn into the prepared tin and bake in a preheated oven, 190°C (375°F), Gas Mark 5, for about 15 minutes until just firm. Turn out onto a wire rack to cool.

3 For the filling, sprinkle the gelatine over the cold water in a bowl and leave for 5 minutes. Grease the sides of a 20 cm/8 inch springform or loose-based cake tin and line with a strip of greaseproof paper. Cut the sponge in half horizontally and place one half in the tin. Stand the bowl of gelatine in a pan of hot water and leave until the gelatine has melted.

4 Melt 175 g/6 oz of the chocolate. Beat the mascarpone in a bowl with the sugar, vanilla essence, yogurt and hot water. Whisking well, gradually pour the gelatine mixture into the mascarpone mixture. Spoon one half into a separate bowl and beat in the chocolate. Turn the chocolate mixture into the tin and level the surface. Cover with the second sponge, then the remaining mascarpone mixture. (If the mascarpone mixture has already started to set, beat in a little hot water.) Level the surface and chill the torte for several hours or overnight.

5 To decorate, remove from the tin and transfer to a serving plate. Remove the greaseproof paper. Melt the remaining chocolate. Using a teaspoon, drizzle the chocolate over the top of the torte. Chill until ready to serve.

Chocolate Cups with Dipped Fruits and Nuts

Melted chocolate, moulded and set in foil cases, makes an impressive container for sweet treats.

Makes: 4

Preparation time: 25 minutes, plus chilling

Cooking time: 5–8 minutes

300 g/10 oz Cadbury's Bournville chocolate, broken into pieces
225 g/7½ oz strawberries
125 g/4 oz red cherries or grapes
50 g/2 oz Brazil nuts

1 Melt 200 g/7 oz of the chocolate. Cut out 4 x 20 cm/8 inch rounds of heavy duty foil. Take 1 circle and mould it around an orange or large apple, fitting it tightly around the base of the fruit and pulling the edges of the foil upright to create a cup shape. Carefully remove the fruit and press the foil cup gently on to a work surface so that it stands upright. Shape the remaining foil in the same way to make 3 more cups.

2 Spoon a little chocolate into 1 foil cup, then spread it over the inside with the back of the spoon. Coat the remaining cups in the same way, using about half the chocolate. Chill for about 10 minutes until beginning to set, then give a second coat with the remaining melted chocolate. Keep the cups in a cool place, or chill for at least

30 minutes until set.

3 Meanwhile, melt the remaining chocolate. Half dip the fruit and nuts in the chocolate cups and leave to set on a sheet of greaseproof paper.

4 Using cool hands, carefully peel the foil away from the chocolate cups, starting at the top and working down to the bottom. Fill with the fruit and nuts and keep in a cool place until ready to serve.

variations
The chocolate cups can also be used as containers for presenting other desserts, such as The Best Chocolate Mousse on page 18, Chocolate Lime Creams on page 24, or even presenting a selection of after dinner chocolates.

Layered Chocolate Marzipan Gâteau

Several layers of rich chocolate sponge, almond paste and brandied apricots give this cake a wonderful flavour. It can be completed a day in advance and kept in a cool place or the refrigerator. If you chill the gâteau, remove it from the refrigerator an hour or so before serving.

Serves: **14**

Preparation time: 40 minutes, plus cooling

Cooking time: 1 hour

150 g/5 oz Cadbury's Bournville chocolate, broken into pieces
75 ml/3 fl oz milk
175 g/6 oz unsalted butter, softened
275 g/9 oz light muscovado sugar
3 eggs, beaten
300 g/10 oz plain flour
1 tablespoon baking powder
150 ml/¼ pint soured cream
FILLING
225 g/7½ oz ready-to-eat dried apricots
½ teaspoon cornflour
4 tablespoons brandy or orange juice
225 g/7½ oz apricot conserve
100 ml/3½ fl oz water plus 1 tablespoon
TO FINISH
750 g/1½ lb golden almond paste
cocoa powder, for dusting
about 8 physalis (cape gooseberries)

1 Grease and line a 23 cm/9 inch cake tin. Melt the chocolate with the milk.
2 Beat together the butter and sugar until pale and creamy. Gradually beat in the eggs, a little at a time, adding a little of the flour if the mixture begins to curdle. Stir in the chocolate mixture. Sift the flour and baking powder into the bowl. Add the soured cream and fold the ingredients together using a large metal spoon. Turn the mixture into the prepared tin and bake in a preheated oven, 180°C (350°F), Gas Mark 4, for about 50 minutes until just firm. Remove from the tin and transfer to a wire rack to cool.

3 For the filling, chop the apricots and put in a small saucepan with 100 ml/3½ fl oz water. Simmer gently for 3–4 minutes until the apricots are soft. Blend the cornflour with 1 tablespoon water and add to the pan with the brandy or orange juice. Cook, stirring, until thickened. Remove from the heat and add half the apricot conserve. Leave to cool.
4 Split the cake horizontally into 3 layers. Place 1 layer on a serving plate and spread half the apricot mixture over the top. Roll out 175 g/6 oz of the almond paste to a 23 cm/9 inch round and lay it over the cake. Add another cake layer, the remaining apricot mixture and another round of almond paste. Add the final cake layer.
5 Melt the remaining apricot conserve and press through a sieve. Spread the conserve over the top and sides of the cake. Thinly roll out the remaining almond paste to a 38 cm/15 inch round. Lay it over the cake, crumpling it up slightly so that it covers the cake in loose folds. Fit the paste around the side and trim off the excess around the base.
6 Dust the cake with cocoa powder. Decorate with the physalis, with their husks peeled back.

variation
Other dried fruits can be used instead of the apricots. Prunes and figs work particularly well.

Bûche de Noël

Cadbury's Flake is perfect for giving cakes a bark-like decoration, as in this French Christmas log. The log can be made a day in advance or it can be frozen. Dust it with icing sugar just before serving.

Serves: **10**

Preparation time: 40 minutes, plus cooling

Cooking time: 20 minutes

3 eggs
75 g/3 oz caster sugar, plus extra for
 sprinkling
50 g/2 oz plain flour
25 g/1 oz cocoa powder
FILLING
150 ml/¼ pint double cream
150 g/5 oz canned sweetened chestnut
 purée
TO DECORATE
150 ml/¼ pint double cream
200 g/7 oz Cadbury's Bournville
 chocolate, broken into pieces
3 Cadbury's Flake
icing sugar, for dusting

1 Grease a 33 x 23 cm/13 x 9 inch Swiss roll tin, line it with paper, then grease the tin. Whisk the eggs and sugar in a heatproof bowl set over a pan of hot water until the mixture leaves a trail when the beaters are lifted from the bowl. Sift the flour and cocoa powder into the bowl. Using a large metal spoon, fold the flour and cocoa into the whisked mixture until just combined.

2 Turn the mixture into the prepared tin and spread it into the corners. Bake in a preheated oven, 180°C (350°F), Gas Mark 4, for about 15 minutes until just firm. Sprinkle a sheet of greaseproof paper with caster sugar and invert the cake on to it. Peel away the lining paper, then roll the sponge up in the fresh paper and leave to cool.

3 For the filling, whip the cream until softly peaking, then fold in the chestnut purée. Unroll the sponge and spread the chestnut cream over the top. (Don't worry if the cake cracks as this won't show once it is reassembled.) Roll the cake back into a log shape. If liked, cut a thick diagonal slice off one end of the cake and attach it to the side to resemble a branch.

4 For the decoration, bring the cream almost to the boil in a small saucepan. Remove from the heat and stir in the chocolate. Leave until melted, then stir until smooth. Leave to cool.

5 Arrange the cake, join side down, on a serving plate. Lightly whip the chocolate cream to thicken it slightly, then spread it over the top and sides of the cake, leaving the ends exposed. Cut the Flake lengthways into long pieces. Press them lightly on to the chocolate cream to decorate, filling in the gaps with smaller pieces of Flake. Dust the log generously with icing sugar and serve.

variation
If you prefer not to use chestnut purée in the filling, simply use whipped cream. A dash of brandy or rum can be added for extra flavour. Alternatively, if you can't get sweetened chestnut purée, use half a 435 g/11¼ oz can unsweetened chestnut purée and beat in 2 tablespoons caster sugar.

Passionfruit Chocolate Torte

A wonderful soft-textured cake, richly laden with tropical fruit and nuts. To save time, use a food processor to chop the chocolate, nuts and dried fruit into small pieces.

Serves: **10**

Preparation time: 20 minutes, plus cooling

Cooking time: about 35 minutes

6 eggs, separated
175 g/6 oz caster sugar
75 g/3 oz fresh white breadcrumbs
1 teaspoon baking powder
100 g/3½ oz blanched almonds, chopped
100 g/3½ oz dried mango or pawpaw, chopped
150 g/5 oz Cadbury's Bournville chocolate, chopped
4 passionfruit
300 ml/½ pint double or whipping cream
1 tablespoon icing sugar

1 Grease and line the base and sides of a 23 cm/9 inch springform tin or cake tin. Whisk the egg yolks with 150 g/5 oz of the sugar until light and creamy.

2 Mix together the breadcrumbs, baking powder, almonds, dried fruit and chocolate and stir into the whisked mixture.

3 Whisk the egg whites until they are stiff, then gradually whisk in the remaining sugar. Using a large metal spoon, fold the egg whites into the chocolate mixture. Turn the mixture into the prepared tin and bake in a preheated oven, 180°C (350°F), Gas Mark 4, for about 35 minutes until only just firm. Cover with a damp tea towel and leave for 10 minutes, then invert the cake on to a wire rack and leave to cool completely.

4 Transfer the cake to a serving plate. Halve 2 of the passionfruit and press the pulp through a sieve to extract the juice. Whip the cream with the icing sugar and passionfruit juice until just peaking. Swirl the mixture over the top of the torte. Remove the pulp from the remaining passionfruit and spoon it over the cream to decorate.

variation
Dried tropical fruit are widely available in supermarkets. If you can't find them, ready-to-eat dried apricots or peaches make a good substitute.

Easter Nest Torte

Cadbury's Mini Eggs nestling on a bed of chocolate shavings make a festive decoration for this richly flavoured Easter cake. The chocolate collar is surprisingly easy to make, yet looks really impressive.

Serves: **12**

Preparation time: 50 minutes, plus cooling and chilling

Cooking time: 25–30 minutes

75 g/3 oz self-raising flour
½ teaspoon baking powder
40 g/1½ oz cocoa powder
125 g/4 oz unsalted butter, softened
125 g/4 oz caster sugar
2 eggs
75 g/3 oz Cadbury's Bournville chocolate, broken into pieces
4 tablespoons orange-flavoured liqueur or orange juice

FILLING
2 teaspoons powdered gelatine
2 tablespoons cold water
3 egg yolks
50 g/2 oz caster sugar
1 teaspoon cornflour
300 ml/½ pint milk
200 g/7 oz Cadbury's Bournville chocolate, broken into pieces
300 ml/½ pint whipping cream

TO DECORATE
150 g/5 oz Cadbury's Dairy Milk chocolate, at room temperature
2 standard packets Cadbury's Mini Eggs

1 Grease a 23 cm/9 inch springform tin or cake tin and line the base. Sift the flour, baking powder and cocoa powder into a bowl. Add the butter, sugar and eggs and whisk well until smooth and creamy. Turn the mixture into the prepared tin, level the surface and bake in a preheated oven, 180°C (350°F), Gas Mark 4, for 20–25 minutes until just firm. Remove from the tin and transfer to a wire rack to cool. Transfer the sponge to a serving plate and drizzle with the liqueur or juice.

2 Make the chocolate collar to go around the edge of the cake. Measure the circumference of the sponge with a piece of string. Cut a strip of greaseproof paper 1 cm/½ inch longer than the string and 6 cm/2½ inches deep. Melt the plain chocolate.

3 Spoon the melted chocolate along the paper strip, spreading it right to the edge along one long side and shaping a slightly wavy line along the other long side about 1.5 cm/⅝ inch away from the edge. Leave 1 cm/¾ inch free of chocolate at one of the ends. Set aside for about 15 minutes until the chocolate has thickened slightly and does not run when it is lifted. Carefully lift the chocolate strip on the paper and secure it around the sponge so the straight edge of the chocolate rests on the plate and the ends of the strip just meet. Chill while making the filling.

4 Sprinkle the gelatine over the cold water in a small bowl and leave to soften. Beat the egg yolks in a bowl with the sugar, cornflour and a little of the milk. Put the remaining milk in a heavy-based saucepan and bring just to the boil. Pour the milk over the egg yolk mixture, whisking well. Return the mixture to the saucepan and cook gently, stirring, until thickened. (Do not allow the mixture to boil or it may curdle.)

5 Remove from the heat and stir in the gelatine until dissolved. Add the chocolate and leave until melted. Stir until smooth, then turn into a bowl. Cover with a piece of greaseproof paper to prevent a skin forming. Leave to cool until just beginning to thicken. Remove the greaseproof paper.

6 Whip the cream until peaking and fold into the chocolate mixture. Turn into the chocolate case on top of the sponge and level the surface. Chill for 1–2 hours until set. Remove the greaseproof paper strip.

7 Using a sharp knife, slice the milk chocolate into long thin shards. If it breaks into brittle pieces, soften it very briefly in the microwave. Lay the chocolate shards on top of the cake to create a nest. Pile the Mini Eggs in the centre to decorate. Chill until ready to serve.

Chocolate Rose Roulade

This perfect roulade is exceptionally moist inside with a crisp crust that cracks a little when the sponge is rolled up. The cream filling is scented lightly with rosewater, but it can be left plain if you prefer. For an extra-special touch, scatter sugared rose petals over the roulade before serving.

Serves: **8**

Preparation time: 20 minutes, plus cooling

Cooking time: 25 minutes

175 g/6 oz Cadbury's Bournville chocolate, broken into pieces
5 eggs, separated
150 g/5 oz caster sugar
extra caster sugar, for sprinkling
300 ml/½ pint whipping cream
2 tablespoons rosewater
1 tablespoon icing sugar
chocolate curls (see page 8), to decorate
extra icing sugar, for dusting

1 Grease and line a 33 x 23 cm/13 x 9 inch Swiss roll tin with greaseproof paper, then grease the paper. Melt the chocolate.
2 Whisk together the egg yolks and sugar until thickened and pale. Stir in the melted chocolate. Whisk the egg whites until stiff. Using a large metal spoon, fold the egg whites into the chocolate mixture. Turn into the prepared tin and spread to the corners. Bake in a preheated oven, 180°C (350°F), Gas Mark 4, for about 20 minutes until risen and just firm.
3 Sprinkle a sheet of greasepoof paper with caster sugar. Invert the sponge on to the paper and peel away the lining paper. Cover with a damp tea towel and leave to cool.
4 Whip the cream with the rosewater and icing sugar until softly peaking. Spread the mixture over the sponge and roll up from a short side. Place the roulade, join side down, on to a serving plate. Scatter chocolate curls over the roulade and dust with icing sugar.

Chocolate Truffle Gâteau

A elegant but simple dessert with a chocolate sponge base and fresh blueberries nestling under a smooth chocolate truffle topping. It keeps well for up to 24 hours.

Serves: **10**

Preparation time: 25 minutes, plus cooling and chilling

Cooking time: about 30 minutes

3 eggs
75 g/3 oz caster sugar
50 g/2 oz plain flour
25 g/1 oz cocoa powder
25 g/1 oz unsalted butter, melted
FILLING
450 ml/¾ pint double cream
250 g/8 oz Cadbury's Bournville chocolate, broken into pieces
4 tablespoons brandy or orange-flavoured liqueur
300 g/10 oz fresh blueberries
cocoa powder, for dusting

1 Grease and line a 23 cm/9 inch springform or loose-based cake tin. Whisk the eggs and sugar in a heatproof bowl set over a pan of hot water until the mixture leaves a trail when the beaters are lifted. Remove from the heat.

2 Sift the flour and cocoa powder into the bowl. Using a large metal spoon, fold in the flour and cocoa. Pour the butter around the edge of the bowl and fold in gently. Turn the mixture into the prepared tin and level the surface. Bake in a preheated oven, 200°C (400°F), Gas Mark 6, for about 25 minutes until just firm to the touch. Transfer the cake to a wire rack and leave to cool completely.

3 For the filling, bring half the cream almost to the boil in a saucepan. Remove from the heat and stir in the chocolate. Leave until melted, then add the remaining cream and the brandy or liqueur and stir until smooth. Leave to cool completely.

4 Clean the cake tin and line the inside with a strip of greaseproof paper. Put the sponge back in the tin and scatter blueberries over the top. Spread the chocolate mixture over the blueberries and level the surface. Chill for at least 1 hour. Carefully remove the cake from the tin and serve generously dusted with cocoa powder.

Chocolate, Meringue and Strawberry Gâteau

Combining an abundance of favourite ingredients, including meringue, chocolate cake, strawberries and cream, this makes a really spectacular cake for a special tea in the summer. Once assembled, it can be kept in the refrigerator for several hours before serving.

Serves: **12**

Preparation time: 30 minutes, plus cooling

Cooking time: about 40 minutes

125 g/4 oz unsalted butter, softened
125 g/4 oz caster sugar
2 eggs
75 g/3 oz self-raising flour
1 teaspoon baking powder
2 teaspoons vanilla essence
25 g/1 oz cocoa powder
MERINGUE
3 egg whites
175 g/6 oz caster sugar
25 g/1 oz flaked almonds
TO FINISH
300 ml/½ pint double cream
100 g/3½ oz Cadbury's Bournville
  chocolate, broken into pieces
225 g/7½ oz strawberries

1 Grease the base and sides of 2 20 cm/8 inch round loose-based sandwich tins and line with nonstick baking parchment.
2 Put the butter, sugar, eggs, flour, baking powder, vanilla essence and cocoa powder in a bowl and beat well until smooth and creamy. Turn the mixture into the prepared tins and level the surface.
3 For the meringue, whisk the egg whites until stiff. Gradually whisk in the sugar, beating well after each addition until the mixture is stiff and glossy. Arrange half the almonds around the inside of the tins so they're flat against the paper, tucking them down between the sponge mixture and the paper.
4 Turn the meringue into the tins. Level the surface and sprinkle with the remaining almonds. Bake in a preheated oven, 180°C (350°F), Gas Mark 4, for about 35 minutes until the meringue is pale golden and just firm. Leave to cool in the tins.
5 Bring 75 ml/3 fl oz of the cream to the boil in a saucepan. Remove from the heat and stir in the chocolate. Leave until melted, then stir until smooth. Transfer to a bowl and leave to cool.
6 Reserve several whole strawberries for the top of the cake. Halve the remainder. Carefully remove the cakes from the tins. Place 1 cake layer on a serving plate. Whip the remaining cream and spread over the cake on the plate. Arrange the strawberries on top. Lightly whip the chocolate cream until slightly thickened, then spread over the cake. Position the second cake on top and decorate with the reserved whole strawberries.

Very Rich Chocolate Gâteau

Dark, rich and classically glossy, this is a seriously indulgent chocolate gâteau. Keep it in a cool place, rather than chilling, otherwise the glaze will set to a matt finish.

Serves: **12–14**

Preparation time: 25 minutes, plus cooling and setting

Cooking time: about 40 minutes

200 g/7 oz Cadbury's Bournville chocolate, broken into pieces
2 tablespoons milk
175 g/6 oz unsalted butter, softened
175 g/6 oz caster sugar
175 g/6 oz ground hazelnuts or almonds
40 g/1½ oz plain flour
5 eggs, separated
3 tablespoons hot water
LIQUEUR SYRUP
25 g/1 oz caster sugar
4 tablespoons brandy or orange- or coffee-flavoured liqueur
GLAZE
5 tablespoons apricot conserve
25 g/1 oz caster sugar
75 ml/3 fl oz water
200 g/7 oz Cadbury's Bournville chocolate, chopped
25 g/1 oz Cadbury's Dairy Milk chocolate, broken into pieces

1 Grease and line a 23 cm/9 inch cake tin. Melt the chocolate with the milk.
2 Put the chocolate mixture, softened butter, sugar, hazelnuts or almonds, flour and egg yolks in a bowl with the hot water and beat until smooth and creamy.
3 Whisk the egg whites in a separate bowl until peaking. Fold one-quarter into the chocolate mixture to lighten it, then fold in the remainder. Turn the mixture into the prepared tin and level the surface. Bake in a preheated oven, 180°C (350°F), Gas Mark 4, for about 30 minutes until just firm. Cover with a damp tea towel and leave to cool in the tin.
4 For the liqueur syrup, put the sugar, brandy or liqueur and 50 ml/2 fl oz water in a small saucepan and heat gently until the sugar dissolves. Bring to the boil and boil rapidly for 1 minute until syrupy. Invert the cake on to a wire rack, remove the lining paper and spoon the syrup over the top.
5 For the glaze, heat the apricot conserve and press through a sieve. Brush over the cake. Heat the sugar in a small, heavy-based saucepan with the water until the sugar has dissolved. Bring to the boil and boil rapidly for 1 minute. Remove from the heat, leave for 1 minute, then stir in the plain chocolate, then leave until melted, stirring frequently. Leave until beginning to thicken. Melt the milk chocolate.
6 Pour the chocolate glaze over the cake, easing it down the side with a palette knife. Using a teaspoon, drizzle the milk chocolate around the top edge of the cake to give a decorative finish. Leave in a cool place to set.

Index